Mario Ratto

"Ma Cuisine.."

for

HOME LINES

GRAFICHE MODIANO - TRIESTE - ITALY

FOREWORD

As an ancient saying rightfully goes, the good cooking may be appreciated and tasted during all ages: when one is young, at the acme of virility and also in the old age.

As a matter of fact, while the sight, the hearing, the sense of touch and the smell tend to dull or somewhat get weaker, the sense of taste is the only and very one that accompanies man until his last decline. Thereby derives the importance that feeding has for all of us.

Different are man's tastes and habits, everchanging too, the climatic conditions, environment, the religious influence, their familial, regional and race traditions, but one thing is well certain that everybody to live must feed oneself and it is also certain that one who knows to choose the different foods and prepare them or blend them in the most suitable way, lives better and more comfortably than those who lower the food preparation to a mere physiological function and need.

With this in mind, the cookery becomes an art and as such it accounts its lovers, its affectionates and connoisseurs.

The food must be easy to prepare, pleasant for the sight, sound and tasty when consumed.

Chef Mario R. Ratto, with a thirty-year experience in the culinary art, does not propose us through this book, the usual recipe collection anyone can find in a common cookbook. Unique in its kind, every recipe is illustrated by a full color picture. The various dishes making up a good dinner have been simplified in such a way that even the unexperienced can find them easy to prepare and nevertheless they turn out to be classical in their display and personalized in their preparation.

We trust that also with this new work, Chef Mario R. Ratto has been able to tell something new, exciting and original in an art so different and so rich of phantasy.

CHEF'S
SALAD
ARISTOCRAT

To serve 6 persons

1/2 lb roast or boiled beef	
1/2 lb roast or boiled chicken	
3 oz Swiss cheese	
2 celery hearts	Oil
1/2 lb fresh mushrooms	Salt
4 1/2 oz radishes	Pepper
4 1/2 oz peppers	Cloves
3/4 oz spring onions	Mustard
1/2 lb tomatoes	Lemon
6 hard-cooked eggs	Parsley
4 lettuce hearts	Mayonnaise

Dice beef, chicken, Swiss cheese and celery. Cut radishes into thin slices, peppers into small strips and finely chop onions. Combine all above ingredients in a salad bowl.

Accurately clean and wash mushrooms then cut them into very thin slices; marinate for half an hour in a plate with oil, salt, pepper and cloves. Add to salad bowl.

Cut tomatoes into thin round slices and remove seeds. Slice hard cooked eggs by means of an egg slicer. Reserve two green lettuce leaves per person, cut hearts into small strips and add to salad bowl.

Dressing: Blend a little French mustard in oil, add lemon juice, finely chopped parsley and some tablespoons mayonnaise as desired. Thoroughly mix and season salad.

Choose a large serving plate, arrange all around edges lettuce leaves. Neatly put tomato slices on lettuce and top them with sliced eggs. Arrange salad in center of platter.

TOMATO
SOUFFLE'

To serve six persons

2 lbs tomatoes
5 1/2 oz butter
1 oz onions
6 mint leaves
1 pinch salt
1 pinch pepper
4 1/2 oz flour
1 dash nutmeg
1/2 teaspoon sugar
3 oz grated Parmesan or Swiss
cheese
1 pint milk
4 eggs

Pare well ripe tomatoes, remove seeds and chop them very finely. Melt 2 oz butter in a pan, add finely chopped onions and sauté without browning. Add tomatoes, salt pepper and sugar. Increase heat and cook until sauce thickens. Remove from heat and add chopped mint leaves. Melt remaining butter in a pan, add flour and stir with a wooden spoon until mixture becomes yellowish, pour boiled milk and whip until mixture becomes creamy and smooth. Add nutmeg and slowly cook for 10 minutes. Take from heat and pour in a bowl. Let become lukewarm then fold in egg yolks, reserving whites, tomato sauce and grated cheese.
Butter a mold or six individual molds, sprinkle with flour so as to form a thin film. Stiffly beat egg whites and fold in the mixture. Pour in mold and bake in moderate oven for 45 minutes, if a large mold is used, or for 20 minutes for individual molds. Cooked soufflé will increase double in bulk. Serve at once.

STUFFED MUSHROOMS LITTLE WHITE HORSE

To serve 6 persons
36 medium sized fresh mushrooms
4 oz butter
1 tarragon sprig
2 cloves garlic
50 snails, canned
1/2 lemon
2 oz parsley
Toast, sized as mushrooms
1 pinch salt
1 pinch pepper

Finely chop garlic, parsley, tarragon and mushrooms stems after having washed the latter and squeezed them dry.
Combine above ingredients with 2 1/2 oz butter, lemon juice salt and pepper. Stir until well blended.
Wash and clean mushrooms caps and put them in a pan with remaining butter. Place caps with hollow-side up arranging a snail in the center. Top snails with half teaspoon each of prepared mixture. Cover pan with aluminium foil or parchment paper and bake in moderate oven for 10 minutes. Prepare hot toasts. Remove from oven and place one mushroom over each toast.
Arrange toasts on platter with napkin and garnish with watercress or a tuft or parsley in the center.

SMALL TOASTS DEL GRANDE STYLE

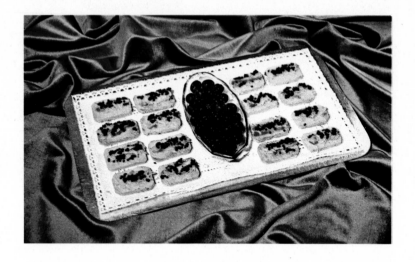

To serve 6 persons

6 1/2 oz crab meat
10 cleaned and boiled shrimps
2 oz butter
1 pinch paprika
1 pinch salt
2 tablespoons Cognac or Brandy
toasted bread
2 oz black caviar
1/2 lb black olives

Press shrimps through a sieve or food chopper. Combine them with butter, salt and paprika. Mix well with a spatula sprinkle Cognac and spread toasts with this mixture.
Top with crab fillets and some pearls of caviar. Cut or trim toasts to the desired size and shape.
Serve on platter with doilies placing in center a cup filled with black olives.

4

SARDINE PEARLS

WITH

PEANUTS

To serve 6 persons
1/2 lb creamed cottage cheese
or ricotta
1/2 lb mashed sardines
1 teaspoon mustard
2 lemons
1 pinch freshly ground pepper
1 pinch paprika
1/2 lb toasted peanuts

Combine creamed cottage cheese, mashed sardines, mustard, lemon juice, pepper and paprika in a bowl. Mix well until blended. Shape mixture into little balls and place them in refrigerator for one hour. Finely chop peanuts and roll in balls.
Serve in small ramekins or heap them on a round plate. Garnish with green leaves.

ROQUEFORT
OR GORGONZOLA
STUFFED CELERY

To serve 6 persons

3 medium sized celery
7 oz Roquefort or Gorgonzola
2 oz butter
1 teaspoon chopped onion
1 teaspoon Worcestershire
Sauce
1 dash paprika
toasted almonds
parsley

Press cheese and butter through a sieve and put mixture in a bowl. Stir with a spatula until creamy. Add chopped onion and Worcestershire Sauce. Fill celery hearts with mixture and dust with paprika. Top larger end of celery with hald toasted almond and smaller end with one parsley leaf. Serve on a plate with napkin.

SMOKED TONGUE
AND
SWISS CHEESE
CANAPES
VILLA D'ESTE

To serve 6 persons

18 thin slices salmi or smoked
tongue
18 thin slices Swiss cheese
3 oz Mayonnaise (Recipe N.
235)
1 teaspoon mustard
Small toasts

Shape ox tongue and toasted bread into 2 inch discs.
Shape Swiss cheese into 1 inch discs.
Spread toasts with a thin layer of mayonnaise flavored with
a pinch of mustard. Arrange a disc of tongue and top with
Swiss cheese. To vary, shape tongue or cheese differently so
that either one or the other will top toasts.
Serve on a platter with doilies and garnish with a tuft of
watercress.

ANCHOVIES
PINK BUTTER
CANAPES

To serve 6 persons

5 1/2 oz unsalted butter
4 1/2 oz tomato ketchup
2 lemons
1 pinch Cayenne pepper or
Tabasco Sauce
Anchovies

Marinate anchovies for one hour in their oil, a few slices of garlic and a little vinegar.
Combine butter, tomato ketchup, lemon juice, pepper or six drops Tabasco in a bowl. Work with a spatula until creamy and pink in color. Spread this mixture on toasts and top with anchovy fillets. To further decorate fill a syringe or a canvas pastry bag with pink butter and squeeze it on anchovies. Serve on a plate with doilies garnishing with a tuft of parsley.

SMALL PUFF
PASTES
REGINELLA

To serve 6 persons

7 oz boiled and chopped chicken
2 oz Mayonnaise (recipe N. 235)
2 oz chopped peppers
2 oz chopped celery hearts
Allspice, 1 pinch
1 pinch grated horseradish
Stuffed olives

Get some small puff pastes currently marketed.
Combine all ingredients except olives and mix throughly.
Fill puff pastes with mixture. Garnish with a slice of stuffed olive. Serve on a plate with napkin.

SMOKED SALMON FOAM BITS

To serve 6 persons

2 large cucumbers
Rye bread
Mustard
36 capers
2 oz Mayonnaise (Recipe N. 235)
7 oz smoked salmon
2 oz butter
1 sprig of dill
1 lemon
1 pinch freshly ground pepper

Finely chop salmon and dill; combine them with butter, lemon juice and pepper. Work with a spatula until foamy.
Pare two cucumbers, cut ends and scoop out pulp by means of a teaspoon. Fill with salmon foam as much as it will go. Refrigerate for 2 hours.
Prepare rye bread toasts. Cut them into round of the same size as cucumbers. Spread with mustard.
Cut cucumbers into discs 1/4 inch thick. Top toasts and decorate with mayonnaise and one caper.
Serve on a plate with napkin. Garnish with a star-shaped lemon and two lettuce leaves.

EGG
CANAPES
THOUSAND
FLOWERS

To serve 6 persons

3 hard cooked eggs
24 small artichokes in oil or radishes
4 1/2 oz Mayonnaise (Recipe N. 235)

3 oz chopped anchovies
2 oz capers
1/2 teaspoon paprika
toasts

Combine mayonnaise, chopped anchovies, capers and paprika in a bowl and mix until creamy. Spread mixture on round toasts. Slice hard cooked eggs with egg slicer and top toasts with an egg slice each. Dot center of egg with remaining mayonnaise mixture and arrange a small opened artichoke or a radish not completely cut into quarters.
To vary, cut eggs lenghtwise into segments. In this case, to have a better display, shape toasts accordingly.
Serve cold on a plate with napkin and garnish with green leaves.

TUNA – FISH CANAPES PHANTASY

To serve 6 persons

7 oz tuna fish in olive oil
1/2 oz Chives or spring onions
2 oz Mayonnaise (Recipe N. 235)
toasted bread
1 lemon
Peanut butter
Pickled onions, in vinegar
White pepper

Finely chop tuna fish and chives or spring onions. Combine them in a bowl with mayonnaise, lemon juice, a dash of white pepper and mix until well blended.
Spread a layer of peanut butter on toasts and another layer of prepared mixture. Cut and trim toasts in various shapes as desired. Top each canapé with one small pickled onion. Serve on a plate with napkin and garnish with green leaves.

GRACIOUSNESS OF QUAILS DIANA

To serve 6 persons

6 quails
2 cans of quail or pheasant
eggs
3 1/2 oz salt pork
12 fresh sage leaves
2 oz butter
2 tablespoons Madeira wine
1 dash Cognac
1 pinch Allspice

Clean quails well. Fill a skewer with quails interposing sage leaves and salt pork slices.
Melt butter in a pan and slowly brown quails for 15 minutes.
Remove and allow to cool. Finely chop all meat. Strain butter in pan and reserve. Sprinkle stock remained in pan with 2 tablespoons of Madeira or Port wine. Scrap bottom and reserve gathered stock. Put chopped quails in a bowl and place it in a larger bowl filled with crushed ice cubes.
Work meat with a spatula for 5 minutes until soft and fluffy.
Gradually add strained butter, reserved stock, a dash of Cognac and a pinch of allspice.
Spread mixture on 2 inch round toasts. Top with a quail egg cut into sixths and arranged flowerlike.
Serve on a plate with napkin and garnish with a tuft of watercress.

CHICKEN SALAD VIVEUR

To serve 6 persons

5 lb chicken
4 1/2 lb mushrooms in olive oil
1/2 lb celery hearts
2 oz oil
2 lemons
salt
1 teasp. pepper
4 1/2 oz Mayonnaise (Recipe N. 235)
2 lettuce hearts
2 tomatoes

Boil chicken and let it cool. Cut meat into thin strips as well as mushrooms and celery hearts. Season with oil, lemon juice, pepper, salt and mayonnaise.
Serve on a platter garnished with lettuce leaves and tomato slices.

BRANDY FLAVORED GOOSE LIVER

Goose liver
Butter
Salt
Paprika
Cognac
Toasts

Dice goose liver. Sauté in a pan with butter, salt and one pinch of paprika, for a few minutes, sprinkle with a few drops of Cognac. Serve at once on toasts well hot.

SMOKED STURGEON ROLLS

Smoked sturgeon
Anchovy fillets
Butter
Pepper
Tarragon leaves
Parsley
Rye bread toasts

Prepare smoked sturgeon slices. Pound with a purée block so as to flatten them. Cut or trim into equal sizes and cover with following mixture:
Finely chop sturgeon bits with an equal amount of anchovy fillets. Put in a bowl and combine with an equal amount of butter. Work with a spatula or spoon until well blended.
Add a pinch of pepper and finely chopped tarragon leaves.
Roll sturgeon slices and arrange onto a crystal platter with a fine bouquet of green parsley in the center.
Serve with thin toasts preferably of rye bread.
To vary use smoked salmon instead of sturgeon.

TOMATOES
WITH
TUNA FISH
IN OLIVE
OIL

Tomatoes, large
Salt
Tuna fish
Mayonnaise (Recipe N. 235)
Capers
Spring onion
Olives

Dip large tomatoes in boiling water for a few minutes, drain and sprinkle with cold water to peel them well. Cut into halves. Gently squeeze and add salt. Arrange tomato halves on a sieve to drain for half hour.
Finely mince tuna, add mayonnaise, a little chopped capers and spring onion. Mix well. Fill tomatoes with mixture and top with a stoned olive.
Serve on a round platter arranging tomato halves on lettuce leaves.

MARINATED CELERY HEARTS

Celery hearts
Salt
Bay leaves
spring onions
Pepper grains
Sugar
Oil, water and white vinegar

Cut celery hearts into 2 1/2 inch strips. Wash them thoroughly and put in a pot. Cover with salted water and heat to boiling for a few minutes. Remove and drain. Arrange boiled celeries in a saucepan, preferably pyrexware, add some bay leaves, spring onions, a few peppergrains and a teaspoon sugar. Cover with a mixture of oil, water and white vinegar.
Let them cook slowly but not for too long in such a way as they remain rather rigid. Allow to cool in a shallow porcelain casserole and serve cold.

APPETIZING FRITTERS NEW FASHION

Flour
Mashed potatoes
Salt
Anchovies, mashed
Frying oil
Butter

With an equal amount of flour and boiled and mashed potatoes, make a dough adding salt as necessary.
Roll cut dough paper thin and cut it into discs of 1 1/2 to 2 inches in diameter. Arrange mashed anchovies in the center of each disc and top with a dot of butter. Join two discs leaving mashed anchovies and butter in the middle and seal edges by pressure. Let stand for a few minutes.
Heat olive oil in a pan and fry discs until golden brown.
Remove with a skimmer and drain. Add more salt.
Serve them preferably hot although they can be appreciated cold too.

HAM ROLLS

Butter
Salt
Rasped horseradish
Cooked ham slices
String bean salad

Combine butter, a quarter of its volume of rasped horseradish and salt in a bowl. Work well with a spatula until creamy and blended.
Spread cooked ham slices with mixture and roll them.
Arrange on small buttered toasts.
Serve with string bean salad seasoned as desired.

CARIBBEAN SEA
OYSTERS

To serve 6 persons

72 oysters
2 lemons
1 glass dry white wine
3 teaspoons A 1 Sauce

Open fresh oysters, discarding opened ones. Drain liquor and reserve it in a container. Gently remove shells and dip mollusks in their liquor. Reserve the largest valve of each oyster and clean it.
Transfer oyster and liquor in a saucepan, add lemon juice, white wine and a pinch of pepper. Cook for 2 minutes and allow to cool in stock. Remove oysters one by one and arrange them on reserved valve. Heat stock to boiling until it becomes of a sirup consistency. Add A 1 Sauce and stir. Coat oysters with sauce. Serve cold and garnish with a tuft of parsley. Buttered rye bread toasts go best with these oysters.

LOBSTER
COTE
OF PEGLI

To serve 6 persons

6 lb live lobster
3 celery hearts
12 artichokes in oil
1/2 lb ripe tomatoes
1 teaspoon mustard

Boil live lobster as usual. Cut it into slices and keep in refrigerator. Combine lobster trimmings with diced celery and artichokes in oil to make a salad.
Put in a salad bowl a glass of fresh tomato juice, made by sieving ripe and peeled tomatoes. Add mustard, one pinch of pepper and a few drops of Worcestershire sauce.
Add salt as desired. Mix well but slowly with a spoon.
Arrange lobster slices on serving plate and season with prepared sauce. Garnish with celery and artichoke salad.

ITALIAN PROSCIUTTO AND MELON
Ham and melon

This delicious hors d'oeuvre is purely Italian.
To serve it cut San Daniele or Parma ham into thin slices.
Choose any kind of melon but be sure to select it just ripe
as it is more perfumed.
Cut melon in any desired shape, namely into slices,
segments, cubes, quarters or balls. If desired sprinkle it with
a mild wine to enhance fragrance. Serve chilled, preferably
on crushed ice arranging ham slices on a separate platter.

ITALIAN PROSCIUTTO AND FIGS
Ham and Figs

A variation on the theme Ham and Melon.
Peel chilled fresh figs and arrange them on a crystal or porcelain serving platter. Garnish with green leaves.
Cut San Daniele or Parma ham into thin slices and arrange separately.
If fresh figs are not available, little toasts spread with honey can be used, their taste being very much like figs.

SOFT
CREAM
BUONGUSTO

To serve 12 persons

1 pint heavy cream
2 oz grated Parmesan cheese
5 1/2 oz Dutch cheese
5 1/2 oz Swiss cheese
2 oz Gorgonzola or Roquefort
24 garden radishes
Crackers

Whip cream until stiff. Fold in grated Parmesan cheese and heap mixture onto a round crystal plate.
Crown with strips of Swiss and Dutch cheeses leaving a space in which to arrange previously washed garden radishes with their stem and leaves. Grate Gorgonzola or Roquefort coarsely and sprinkle over cream. Serve with crackers.

QUICK
CHEESE FONDUE

To serve 3 persons

3 oz grated Parmesan or Swiss
cheese
1/2 teaspoon cornstarch or
arrowroot
2 egg yolks
1/2 pint milk
1 pinch salt
1 pinch paprika or white
pepper
Toasts
1 clove of garlic (optional)

Combine in a bowl grated cheese, cornstarch, salt, paprika and egg yolks. Boil milk and add to mixture beating with a whip. Pour in saucepot and keep on stirring with a wooden spoon or spatula. Heat and cook for a few minutes until fondue is thickened, frequently stirring. Remove from heat and serve. If fondue is not served at once, be sure to keep it in bain-marie.

Variations:

For a Cocktail. Arrange fondue in a suitable bowl and place it in bain-marie. Serve along with a tray of small diced toasts pierced by a toothpick and invite self service. Guests will take a dice of toast and will dip it into fondue.

For a Lunch. Serve fondue into individual shirred egg dishes. Separately prepare toasts rubbed with garlic.

For a dinner. Just add some truffle slices to fondue or sliced mushrooms sautéed in butter and sprinkled with finely chopped parsley. Serve with puff pastes.

Hamburgers. Broil or grill hamburgers the usual way. Coat them with fondue.

FRESH MUSHROOM
SALAD
TO LOVE

To serve 6 persons

1 lb fresh mushrooms
1 stick cinnamon
6 cloves
3 lemons
1 clove of garlic
3 oz olive oil
toasts
1 pinch white pepper
5 1/2 oz Swiss cheese
Salt as desired
5 1/2 oz smoked ox tongue
6 lettuce leaves
2 ripe tomatoes

Carefully clean and wash mushrooms. Cut them into very thin slices. Arrange in a casserole (preferably pyrexware) add lemon juice, cinnamon stick, cloves, olive oil, salt and pepper. Gently stir and allow to marinate for one hour.
Cut Swiss cheese into thin slices and tongue into small dice. Arrange lettuce leaves all around serving platter and top with tomato slices. Mix Swiss cheese and mushrooms and arrange salad in center of platter. Top with diced tongue.

CHAMPAGNE LENTIL SOUP

To serve 12 persons

1 lb lentils
1/2 lb potatoes
4 1/2 oz tomato purée
3 oz salt pork
1 oz oil
5 1/2 oz onions
1 sprig thyme
1 teaspoon black pepper
salt as desired
4 quarts water
1 oz butter
1 tablespoon red vinegar

Soak lentils in lukewarm water for a few hours. Heat salt pork and oil in a saucepot until slightly brown.
Add diced onions and allow to brown for 10 minutes then combine lentils and pared potatoes allowing them to gain flavor for a couple of minutes. Pour water and add thyme. Cover and cook for one hour. Add tomato purée and simmer for one hour longer or until lentils are well done.
Take from heat and press through a sieve or force through food chopper. Return to saucepot and heat to boiling for two minutes adding salt, pepper and diced butter. Sprinkle vinegar and simmer until soup is creamy.
Serve with small toasts or croutons. Open a bottle of Champagne in front of guests and sprinkle one tablespoon on each serving.

ONION
SOUP PIGALLE

To serve 12 persons

5 1/2 oz butter
4 lbs onions
3 oz carrots
3 oz mushrooms
3 quarts broth
salt as desired
1 teaspoon pepper
24 French bread croutons
1 dash of paprika
2 oz grated Parmesan or Swiss
cheese
1 glass Sherry

Melt 4 1/2 oz butter in a casserole, add finely sliced onions, grated carrots, chopped mushrooms and salt. Cook slowly for 15 minutes constantly stirring until onions begin browning.

Add broth or water with meat extract. Heat to boiling and cook on high heat for another 15 minutes. Add Sherry and stir.

Serve preferably in individual stew pots or consommé cups. Just before serving put soup and two croutons per person in oven for a few minutes until slightly au gratin.

Croutons: Cut bread into half-inch slices. Arrange in a frying pan with remaining melted butter and brown on both sides. Sprinkle with Parmesan and paprika.

GENOESE MINESTRONE

To serve 12 persons

1/2 lb dried white beans
3 quarts water
1/2 lb cabbage
1/2 lb potatoes
4 1/2 oz celery
1/2 lb rice or 12 oz small

macaroni
1/2 lb zucchini
1/2 lb peas, shelled
1/2 lb Windsor or broad beans
1/2 lb eggplants
1/2 lb green beans
4 1/2 oz basil leaves, fresh
3 oz piquant cheese or 5 1/2

oz Parmesan
1 1/2 oz garlic
1/2 lb olive oil
1 pinch pepper
salt as desired

Soak dried beans overnight. Cook them in water. Add salt and pepper. Finely slice all fresh vegetables, except basil and drop in boiling water. Continue cooking for half hour over high heat. Add rice or small macaronis and allow to cook for 15 to 20 minutes longer. Two minutes before removing add genoese pesto.

Pesto: Combine basil, grated cheese, a pinch of salt and garlic in a mortar and pound with pestle until finely shredded. Blend in oil and a ladle of soup and add to minestrone stirring well.

An electric mixer or food chopper can be used instead of mortar. Dried basil, if used, should be soaked in lukewarm water for 10 minutes.

To vary, prepare minestrone with any kind of fresh vegetables in season, but be sure to drop vegetables in boiling water.

LOBSTER
SOUP DANIELA

To serve 12 persons

5 1/2 oz olive oil
2 oz onions
1 oz garlic
2 oz celery
4 lbs lobster
1 glass dry white wine
1/2 lb ripe tomatoes
4 quarts water
salt as desired
1 teaspoon white pepper
12 oz small pasta
1 sprig tarragon

Heat oil in a saucepan and sauté sliced onions, sliced celery and whole garlic cloves until golden brown.
Cut lobster head lenghtwise and tail crosswise and arrange in saucepan. Stew for a few minutes then sprinkle with white wine. Let evaporate completely and add minced tomatoes and salt. Cover and cook for 10 minutes then add water. Cover and cook for another 1/2 hour or until lobster is done.
Strain stock through cheesecloth. Remove lobster meat from shell and dice. Return lobster meat to strained stock and reheat to boiling. Add pasta and cook for 5 minutes. Add pepper and finely chopped tarragon leaves. Serve hot.

CHICKEN
AND RICE
SOUP
ROMAGNA
STYLE

To serve 12 persons

12 oz leeks
1 lb cabbage
2 1/2 lbs chicken
3 oz salt pork
3 1/2 oz butter
4 quarts water
salt as desired
1 teaspoon pepper, white
12 oz rice

Combine chopped salt pork, sliced leeks and 2 oz butter in a saucepot. Stew for 5 minutes. Add boneless and coarsely chopped chicken. Allow to brown for 5 minutes, add water and salt. Heat to boiling for 20 minutes and add finely sliced cabbage and rice. Continue cooking over high heat for about 20 minutes or until rice is done. Add pepper, more salt as necessary and remaining butter cut into pieces.

RICH
CONSOMME'
DERBY

To serve 12 persons
6 lbs ground lean beef
2 oz carrots
4 1/2 oz celery
3 oz onions
5 1/2 oz ripe tomatoes
1 gal water
12 white pepper grains
salt as desired

Put coarsely ground beef in a saucepot, cover with cold water and let stand for about 1 hour in a cool place.
Stir meat every 15 minutes. Slowly heat to boiling constantly stirring. As water is boiling stop stirring and skim fat from surface. Add vegetables, salt, pepper and simmer for 2 hours.
Strain consommé through cheesecloth, very delicately and without touching meat so as consommé remains clear. If desired add Port wine or Sherry to flavor, in the proportion of 1 tablespoon per person.
Serve hot or cold in consommé cups.

FLORENCE STYLE SOUP

34

To serve 12 persons

2 lbs white dried beans
1/2 lb cabbage
2 lbs potatoes
1/2 tablespoon marjoram
5 1/2 oz grated Parmesan cheese
1 sprig fresh sage
5 1/2 quarts water
5 1/2 oz leeks
5 1/2 oz celery
2 cloves garlic
1/2 lb olive oil
salt as desired
1 teaspoon black pepper
2 to 3 French bread slices per person

Soak beans for a few hours in lukewarm water. Drain and cook in 5 1/2 quarts water adding whole garlic, sage sprig and 2 oz olive oil. Remove from heat and reserve half of beans in a bowl. Remove sage and garlic and force beans and broth through a sieve.

Slightly brown chopped leeks in a saucepot with remaining oil. Add sliced potatoes, celery and cabbage. Stew for 10 minutes then add strained beans. Continue cooking over high heat for half hour then add whole reserved beans, finely chopped marjoram, grated cheese, salt and pepper. Cook for another 5 minutes and serve with toasts.

PEA SOUP CAMPO DEI FIORI

To serve 12 persons

2 lbs fresh peas, shelled
7 oz lean or fat ham
3 oz butter
5 1/2 oz spring onions
5 1/2 oz celery
5 1/2 oz carrots
3 quarts water
1 sprig fresh mint or basil
1 teaspoon black pepper
French bread
salt as desired

Combine minced ham, half butter, finely chopped onions, celery and carrots in a casserole. Slowly brown for 10 minutes. Cover with water and heat to boiling. Add peas. Simmer for half hour then add finely chopped mint or basil, remaining butter, salt and pepper. Serve with small toasts browned in butter or in bacon drippings. The latter will enhance flavor.

MINESTRONE LOMBARD STYLE

To serve 12 persons

5 1/2 oz leeks
5 1/2 oz celery
1 lb potatoes
5 1/2 oz carrots
12 oz tomatoes or 2 oz tomato extract
1 lb cabbage
1 lb fresh red beans or 1/2 lb dried
1/2 lb rice
5 1/2 oz butter or salt pork
4 1/2 oz grated Parmesan cheese
2 oz parsley
1 clove garlic
2 oz oil
1 gal water
1 pinch white pepper
salt as desired

Wash and cut leeks into slices crosswise. Combine leeks, 3 1/2 oz sliced salt pork and 2 oz oil in a saucepan. Sauté without browing for about 5 minutes. Add celery, potatoes and carrots cut into small strips and allow to gain flavor for 15 minutes. Add peeled and minced tomatoes or tomato extract and continue cooking for another 5 minutes over moderate heat.
Cover with water and increase heat continuing cooking for 3/4 hour. Add cabbage and separately cooked beans. 5 minutes after add rice and allow cooking for 15 minutes longer.
Chop remaining salt pork, parsley and garlic as finely as possible and add to soup. Finish cooking for another 5 minutes, fold in Parmesan and pepper and serve.

LINGUINI WITH EGG DROPS VILLA DORIA

To serve 12 persons

1 lb noodles (linguini or vermicelli)
salt as desired
6 1/2 oz oil
2 oz garlic
5 1/2 oz grated Parmesan cheese
1/2 oz fresh marjoram
1 teaspoon allspice
3 eggs
3 1/2 quarts water

Combine water, squeezed whole garlic, oil and salt in a pot. Heat to boiling for 5 minutes and remove garlic.
Break noodles into small pieces and drop into the pot.
Allow to cook for 12 minutes. Combine eggs, grated Parmesan, allspice and finely chopped marjoram in a mixing bowl. Work with a fork until well blended and add to the pot. Finish cooking for 2 minutes and serve.
If dried marjoram is used, soak it in lukewarm water for 10 minutes.

CREAM

basis recipe

To serve 12 persons

1 1/2 quart veal or chicken broth
1 quart milk
4 1/2 oz rice flour
4 1/2 oz leeks
1 pint heavy cream
3 oz butter
1/2 oz salt

Prepare broth in the usual way.
Combine half butter and finely chopped leeks in a pot. Stew for 10 minutes without browning and pour broth. Heat to boiling. Blend rice flour and cold milk and pour in boiling broth. Stir until boiling is resumed. Cook for 1 1/2 hour. Strain through cheesecloth or through a fine mesh strainer. Reheat and add salt. As boiling is resumed remove from heat and place in bain-marie if it not used immediately.
Fold in cream and remaining butter gradually and constantly stirring.
Endless are the variations that can be made using this basis recipe. Add a pea purée, carrots, asparagus, spinach or any other fresh or frozen vegetable. Be sure to add in any case 1/2 lb of strained vegetables.

38

SAVOY SOUP

To serve 12 persons

1/2 lb leeks
2 lbs potatoes
1 lb cabbage
4 1/2 oz carrots
1/2 lb sausage
4 quarts broth
2 1/2 oz grated Swiss cheese
4 1/2 oz butter
5 fennel seeds
Salt and pepper as desired
Slices of bread

Dice leeks. Sauté in a pot with half butter and fennel seeds without browning. Dice potatoes, carrots and cabbage and add to the pot. Simmer for 10 minutes and pour broth.
Boil sausage separately, drain and cool under cold water.
Peel sausage and cut it into small cubes roughly the same size as vegetables. Add to the soup and cook for about 3/4 hour. Add salt and pepper.
Butter a frypan and arrange bread slices. Dust with grated cheese and dot with remaining butter. Place in oven until golden brown and serve with soup.

BEEF AND NOODLES SOUP

To serve 12 persons

2 lbs beef for soup
Salt as desired
1 teaspoon black pepper
5 1/2 oz celery
4 1/2 oz carrots
1/2 lb ripe tomatoes
5 1/2 oz spring onions
1/2 lb potatoes
1/2 lb cabbage
2 oz parsley
1/2 lb noodles (spaghetti or vermicelli)
2 oz butter
1 sprig thyme

Sauté beef cut into half inch cubes in a saucepan with butter. Add spring onions cut into 1 inch strips. Allow to brown. Heat 2 1/2 quarts water to boiling, add browned beef and onion, sprig thyme and peeled tomatoes cut into slices lengthwise. Cook for 1 hour. Cook cabbage separately for one minute. Cut celery, carrots, potatoes and cabbage into small strips and add to soup.
Cook for another half hour then add noodles broken into 1 inch pieces. Finish cooking for another 10 minutes and remove. Coarsely chop parsley leaves and fold in with soup adding salt and pepper.

CHILLED TOMATO CREAM SAN MARZANO

To serve 12 persons

4 lbs ripe tomatoes
5 1/2 oz olive oil
1/2 oz freshly ground black pepper
12 oz cucumbers
4 1/2 oz carrots
2 oz Gorgonzola or Roquefort
3 1/2 oz bread crumbs
1/2 glass vinegar
Salt as desired
1 oz onion
1/2 oz sugar

Dip ripe tomatoes in boiling water for 2 minutes and rinse them under cold water to peel them easily. Cut them into halves lengthwise and remove seeds. Choose three fine halves and reserve. Press remaining tomatoes through a sieve and combine them with salt, olive oil, pepper, sugar, vinegar and bread crumbs. Add as much bread crumbs to reach the desired consistency. Clean and wash onion, carrots, cucumbers and together with reserved tomato halves cut into small dice and fold in with soup.
Serve with small toasts or crackers spread with a thin layer of gorgonzola.
To speed up preparation, use canned tomato juice instead of ripe tomatoes. Omit sugar.

LETTUCE
AND
LASAGNA SOUP

To serve 12 persons

3 lbs lettuce
1 lb dried lasagnas
3 oz oil
3 oz butter
salt as desired
1 teaspoon pepper
1/2 lb spring onions
4 quarts beef or chicken broth
grated cheese

Sauté chopped spring onions in a saucepot with oil for 5 minutes without browning. Add lettuce previously washed and cut into thin strips. Simmer for a few minutes to gain flavor and pour broth. Heat to boiling then add lasagnas. Finish cooking for about 15 minutes. Add butter, salt and pepper. Sprinkle with grated cheese as desired.

CLASSICAL
CREAM
GERMINY

To serve 12 persons

5 1/2 oz sorrel
12 egg yolks
1/2 pint heavy cream
2 quarts broth
2 oz butter
1 teaspoon white pepper

Stew sorrel leaves in butter for a few minutes. Combine sorrel, egg yolks, heavy cream, and pepper in a soup bowl. Mix well and pour boiling broth gradually just before serving, constantly stirring.
Match-like puff pastes and small croutons are the best to go with it.

BARLEY

SOUP

GIARDINIERA

To serve 12 persons
1/2 lb barley pearls
4 1/2 oz carrots
5 1/2 oz celery
4 1/2 oz leeks
1/2 lb potatoes
salt as desired
1 teaspoon white pepper
1/2 pint milk
3 1/2 oz butter

Soak barley pearls in water for a few hours. Drain and put
in a pot with 3 1/2 quarts water. Cover and heat to boiling
then simmer for about 2 hours. Dice carrots, leeks, celery,
potatoes and add to the pot. Add salt and finish cooking for
another half hour over high heat.
Remove, add pepper, butter and milk. Stir well and serve.

FRESH
FRUIT
CREAM SUSYNA

To serve 12 persons

1 lb apples
1/2 lb plums or prunes
1 lb peaches
1 glass white wine
1 pinch powdered cinnamon
2 oz heavy cream
12 fresh mint leaves
1 lb pears
1/2 lb oranges
1/2 lb grapes
2 1/2 oz cornstarch or arrowroot
1/2 lb sugar
4 oz whipped cream
12 cherries in Maraschino

Clean and pare fruits. Put in a pot preferably pyrexware or enameled. Cover with 4 quarts water, add sugar, orange juice and three pieces of orange rind. Heat to boiling and cook for 30 minutes. Remove orange rinds and force all the fruit through a sieve. Return to pot and reheat strained fruit to boiling. Blend cornstarch in white wine and pour mixture in boiling pot. Two minutes after boiling is resumed remove from heat and add cinnamon and unwhipped heavy cream. Stir and allow to cool. Serve in colorful cups.
Just before serving put whipped cream in a syringe and decorate each portion with a dot of cream. Top with a mint leaf and a cherry in Maraschino or stoned fresh cherry with its stem.

FROG SOUP GALLEANI STYLE

To serve 12 persons

5 1/2 oz butter
2 oz carrots
2 oz celery
2 lbs frog legs
3 quarts water or broth
1 teaspoon white pepper
1/2 oz salt
2 oz onions
5 fresh sage leaves
1/2 lb mushrooms
1/2 lb tomatoes
4 1/2 oz heavy cream
Croutons

Chop onions, celery and carrots and brown in a pot with 3 1/2 oz butter for 5 minutes. Add cleaned mushrooms and frog legs. Cook until frog's stock is completely evaporated. Add shredded tomatoes, water or broth and sage. Cover and simmer for one hour. Force through a sieve or food chopper. Reheat to boiling and add salt and pepper. Reduce heat and fold in cream and remaining butter constantly stirring.
Serve with toasted or fried croutons.

BORSCHT SOUP

To serve 12 persons

3 lbs beetroots, well ripe
1/2 lb onions
1 oz sugar
5 caraway seeds or fennel
1/2 oz horseradish
1 tablespoon vegetable extract
5 1/2 oz yoghourt or sour cream
4 quarts water
2 lbs ripe tomatoes
4 lemons
1/2 oz salt
1 tablespoon vinegar
1 oz cornstarch or arrowroot

Pare beets, wash and cut them into slices. Combine sliced beets, caraway or fennel seeds in a pot, add water vinegar and salt. Cook until done. Force beets and water through a sieve. Reheat to boiling then add cornstarch and vegetable extract blended in water. Allow to boil for one minute longer, transfer in a bowl and allow to cool.

Press tomatoes through a sieve. Force twice onions through food chopper. Gather chopped onions on a napkin and wring it to remove onion juice. Add to beetroot cream together with lemon juice, sugar and rasped horseradish. Fold in yoghourt or sour cream. Serve with small puff pastes.

Process can be abbreviated using canned ingredients such as beetroots and tomato juice.

SHERRY FLAVORED RED BEAN SOUP

To serve 12 persons

1 lb red beans
1/2 lb potatoes
4 1/2 oz salt pork
1 oz oil
1 oz butter
4 1/2 oz onions
4 1/2 oz celery
4 1/2 oz rice
1 tespoon black pepper
3 1/2 oz Sherry wine
salt as desired
4 quarts water

Soak red beans in lukewarm water for a few hours. Boil slowly in water for 3/4 hour. Pare potatoes and cut them into halves then add to pot. Chop salt pork and put in a saucepan with oil, diced onions and celery. Brown for ten minutes then add to soup. Continue cooking for another 3/4 hour. Separately cook rice in salted water for 20 minutes and drain. As beans are done, remove and press contents of the pot through a sieve or food chopper adding a little salt. Reheat to boiling adding pepper and rice. Remove and add diced butter and Sherry. Serve at once or keep in bain-marie.

COLD
VEGETABLE
CREAM
OLD SPAIN

To serve 12 persons

4 lbs ripe tomatoes
1 oz onions
1 clove garlic
3 oz peppers
1 oz spring onions
1/2 oz sugar
4 1/2 oz cucumbers
1 teaspoon black pepper
1 pinch paprika
3 lemons
1/2 lb olive oil
4 oz Sherry wine
salt as desired

Dip ripe tomatoes in boiling water for 2 minutes. Rinse them in cold water to peel them easily. Remove seeds and reserve two of the finest tomatoes to be cut into dice.
Press remaining tomatoes through a sieve or food chopper. Clean onions, garlic, spring onions, peppers, cucumbers and chop them very finely. For best results use an electric mixer with chopping blade until creamy. Add to sieved tomatoes together with lemon juice, pepper, paprika, Sherry wine, olive oil, salt and sugar. Mix well and add diced tomatoes. Chill and serve. Garnish with a stalk of fresh celery. Prepare garlic flavored croutons if desired.
Use tomato juice instead of ripe tomatoes.

RICE AND CHICKEN LIVERS SOUP

To serve 12 persons

1 lb chicken livers
4 quarts broth
12 oz rice
2 oz parsley
1/2 oz pepper
3 oz butter
3 oz grated cheese

Heat to boiling broth with rice. Separately boil chicken livers for 1 minute. Drain and cool under running water. Cut into dice and add to broth. Continue cooking for 2 minutes. Add pepper, parsley, butter and grated cheese. Stir well and serve.

CHICK PEAS

SOUP

LIGURIAN STYLE

To serve 12 persons

1 1/2 lbs chick peas
4 quarts water
6 1/2 oz olive oil
1/2 lb spring onions
1 lb green beets
2 oz parsely
5 1/2 oz grated cheese
1/2 oz allspice
salt as desired
Croutons, toasted or fried

Soak chick peas in lukewarm water for a few hours. Drain and wash. Put them in a pot with water and 2 oz olive oil. Heat to boiling and cook for 1 1/2 hour or until they are done.
Sauté chopped onions in remaining oil add finely chopped parsley leaves, finely sliced beets and stew for 10 minutes. Add to cooked chick peas and continue boiling for 10 minutes longer. Add salt, allspice and grated cheese.
Serve with croutons.

CREME VICHYSSOISE

To serve 12 persons

4 1/2 oz leeks
2 lbs potatoes
1 oz chives
7 oz heavy cream
1 oz rice flour
2 oz butter
2 oz salt pork
4 quarts veal or chicken broth
or water
1 teaspoon pepper
3/4 oz salt
3 egg yolks

Wash leeks and cut them into thin slices. Sauté in a pot with chopped salt pork and butter.
Wash and pare potatoes, cut them into pieces and add to the pot. Dust with rice flour and allow to stew for a few minutes. Stir and gradually add broth. Heat to boiling and simmer for 3/4 hour. Press through a sieve or food chopper and reheat to boiling. Remove and add salt and pepper. Whip egg yolks together with heavy cream and fold in with soup. Add chopped chives and stir. Serve either hot or cold.

WHITE CLAM
SAUCE

To serve 12 persons

6 lbs little neck clams
5 1/2 oz olive oil
2 oz garlic
2 oz parsley
5 1/2 oz dry white wine
1 pinch crushed pepper

Thoroughly scrub clam shells under running water with a brush. Finely chop parsley leaves and garlic. Heat 1 oz olive oil in a saucepan, when oil is well hot put in clams and white wine. Cover and keep over high heat until clams open. Remove as shells are open, since clams do not have to be cooked but merely open and release liquor. By means of a skimmer transfer clams on a plate. Remove mollusks and cut them into four pieces. Delicately strain clams liquor through cheesecloth or through a fine mesh strainer. Do not shake pan so that any sand or impurity remains on bottom. Clean saucepan and heat remaining oil adding chopped garlic and parsley, crushed pepper or 1 teaspoon black pepper.
Brown for a few minutes then add reserved strained clam liquor. Simmer until almost sirupy. Remove from heat and add clams without cooking any further.
Use to season vermicelli or spaghetti.
Canned clams can also be used, but of course flavor is beyond comparison using fresh clams.

MEAT SAUCE

To serve 12 persons

2 oz butter
4 1/2 oz olive oil
2 oz carrots
2 oz celery
3 oz onions
1 lb lean beef
1/2 lb pork meat, fat and lean
3 oz tomato purée
2 bay leaves
salt as desired
1 teaspoon black pepper
1 pinch cinnamon
1 pinch sugar
5 1/2 oz red wine

Force carrots, celery and onions through food chopper. Coarsely ground meat. Heat 2 oz olive oil in a frypan and add ground meat. Brown until fair golden.

Combine butter and remaining oil in a casserole, heat until frothy and add mixture of chopped carrots, celery and onions; add bay leaves and allow to brown slightly. Add sautéed meat. Let stand for a few minutes then sprinkle with red wine. Stir until evaporated. Add tomato purée and continue stirring for a few minutes. Cover with water half inch above meat. Add a pinch of salt, pepper, powdered cinnamon, sugar and stir. Cover and simmer for 2 hours occasionally stirring. At this time sauce should be reasonably thick. Should it be too liquid, remove cover and let evaporate to the desired consistency. On the contrary add water gradually to keep sauce from overthickening.

Remove from heat, skim surface if it is too fat.

Use to season any kind of noodles.

SAUCE
CACCIATORA

To serve 12 persons

1 lb mushrooms
3 oz olive oil
2 cloves garlic
1 teaspoon black pepper
1 pinch origan
1 lb basil flavored tomato pulp
(Recipe N. 63)
1 lb meat gravy (Recipe N. 59)
1 lemon
salt as desired
1 oz parsley

Clean mushrooms and cut them into thin slices. Sprinkle with the juice of one lemon to prevent darkening and stir. Heat oil and chopped or whole garlic in a saucepan.
Allow to brown then remove garlic if whole. Add mushrooms, salt, pepper origan and allow to brown for a few minutes.
Pour tomato sauce and meat gravy and cook for 5 minutes.
Add finely chopped parsley leaves.
Excellent for scaloppini, small beef medallions, chicken cacciatora and any kind of fresh noodles.

SAUCE
MARINARA

To serve 12 persons

4 lbs ripe tomatoes
1/2 lb olive oil
2 oz garlic
2 oz parsley
1 teaspoon black pepper
1 pinch origan
3 oz tomato purée
1/2 oz salt

Dip tomatoes in boiling water for 2 minutes and rinse under cold running water to peel them easily. Chop them. Heat oil in a saucepan and add chopped garlic. Sligthly brown then add chopped parsley and origan. One minute after add tomato purée, salt, pepper and chopped tomatoes, Stir well. Cook on high heat until sauce reaches the desired consistency.
Excellent to season any kind of noodles or combined with clams, oysters, etc.

MEAT
SAUCE
WITH
MUSHROOMS

To serve 12 persons
1 lb fresh or canned mushrooms
2 cloves garlic
3/4 oz parsley
2 oz oil or butter
1 lb meat sauce (Recipe N. 54)
salt as desired

Clean mushrooms and cut into thin slices or cubes.
Heat oil or butter in a pan and add chopped garlic.
Slightly brown then add mushrooms and a pinch of salt.
Allow to cook for 10 minutes. Finely chop parsley and sprinkle over mushrooms. Combine mixture with an equal amount of meat sauce. Serve on any kind of pastas.

SAUCE
FINANZIERA

To serve 12 persons

1/2 lb sweetbreads
4 1/2 oz butter
1 oz onion
1/2 lb pork and veal meats
1/2 lb fresh or canned mushrooms
5 1/2 oz fresh peas, shelled or
canned
1/2 lb boneless chicken meat
1 lb meat gravy (Recipe N. 59)
4 oz Madeira or Marsala
1 teaspoon flour
salt as desired
1 pinch pepper

Soak sweetbreads in cold water for 3 to 4 hours changing water twice or three times during that period. Drain and cover with fresh cold water. Heat to boiling for 10 minutes.
Drain, cool and cut into half inch cubes.
Chop onion. Force pork and veal meats through food chopper, add salt and pepper. Mix thoroughly and shape into balls large as a hazelnut. Clean mushrooms and cut them into half inch cubes. Dice chicken meat.
Scald meat gravy in a casserole. Combine butter, chopped onion and diced chicken in a saucepan and slowly cook for 10 minutes. Add mushrooms and as they begin to brown, reduce heat, allow to evaporate then add meat balls. Brown for 5 minutes and add sweetbreads. Stir for a few minutes then dust with flour. Delicately stir for another few minutes, sprinkle with Madeira or Marsala wines then fold in meat gravy and peas. Allow to boil for 2 minutes, add salt and pepper as desired. Remove and serve with noodles, rice, corn meal pudding, lasagnas, etc.

RED CLAM SAUCE

To serve 12 persons

1 lb Sauce Marinara (Recipe
N. 56)
1 lb White Clam Sauce (Recipe
N. 53)

Blend sauce Marinara and white clam sauce in equal
amounts.
Heat to boiling for 2 minutes about.
Use to season spaghetti, linguini, boiled rice, omelets,
shirred or scrambed eggs.

LOBSTER SAUCE

To serve 12 persons

4 lbs lobster
1 oz garlic
3 oz oil
1 teaspoon salt
1 teaspoon black pepper
1 1/2 oz Cognac or Brandy or
4 oz dry white wine
1 1/2 lb Sauce Marinara

Method 1. Cut lobster lenghtwise, remove all meat and cut into half inch cubes. Sauté chopped garlic in oil in a saucepan then add lobster, salt and pepper. Cover and cook for 15 minutes. Fold in sauce Marinara and heat to boiling for 1 minute.

Method 2. Cut lobster and cook as in method 1. Heat 1 oz oil in a saucepan then arrange lobster head, shell, and claws cracked into pieces. Allow to brown for 5 minutes.
Sprinkle with brandy or white wine and let evaporate completely. Add marinara sauce and a cup of water. Cover and cook for 30 minutes and force through a sieve squeezing well head, shell and cracked claws. Combine strained sauce to lobster pieces and heat to boiling for 2 minutes.
Serve with pilaff rice and any kind of noodles.

SEA FOOD SAUCE

It is a variation of sauce Marinara, Recipe N. 56.
Combine one or more pieces of assorted sea food such as clams, calamaries, lobster, shrimps, muscles, crab meat, polyps, scallops, oysters, crawfish, etc.
Clean and shell sea food as usual then sauté or cook them in oil adding one or more squeezed whole cloves of garlic to be removed after cooking.
Combine half amount of assorted sea food in proportion to sauce. That is, using one pound of sauce Marinara add half pound of assorted and cleaned sea food.
Chop or slice all sea food to half inch pieces leaving small mollusks whole.
Cooking time of course varies for the different kinds of sea food used. Clams, oysters and muscles require only a few minutes, just the time to open and release liquor to be strained, reserved and added to sauce.
Calamaries and polyps require half hour cooking well covered until tender. They should then be allowed over heat uncovered until liquor is evaporated. Diced lobster require 10 minutes cooking. Crab meat 4 minutes.
Shrimps and scallops 5 minutes.
Combine all precooked sea food with sauce Marinara and allow to cook for 2 minutes longer.
Serve with spaghetti, boiled or baked rice, linguini, etc.

MUSHROOM
SAUCE

To serve 12 persons

3 oz oil
1 oz garlic
1 teaspoon pepper
1 pinch salt
1/2 lb mushrooms, fresh or canned
1 lb strained tomato sauce
(Recipe N. 60)
1 lemon

Accurately clean mushrooms scraping them with a knife.
Rinse under cold water, rub and pat them dry.
Put them on chopping board, sprinkle with the juice of one lemon, stir and chop very finely with a knife.
Brown oil and squeezed garlic in a pan and add mushrooms constantly stirring until sautéed. Add salt and pepper and remove garlic. Add tomato sauce and heat to boiling for 2 minutes.
Excellent to season egg noodles, spinach noodles, lasagnas, etc.

SAUCE A LA CARUSO

To serve 12 persons

3 oz butter or oil
2 cloves garlic
1 lb chicken livers
1 lemon
1 lb basil flavored tomato pulp
(Recipe N. 63)

Cut chicken livers into halves, clean them well and wash in cold water with the juice of one lemon. Drain and pat them dry with a napkin.
Heat oil or butter in a frypan then add finely chopped garlic. Allow to brown slightly and add chicken livers. Cook over high heat for 4 minutes. Pour tomato pulp and let boil for 2 minutes. Add salt if necessary.
Serve with any kind of noodles and rice.

SCARPARIELLA SAUCE

To serve 12 persons

1 lb sauce Marinara (Recipe N.
56)
3 oz black olives
3 oz green olives
1 pinch origan
1 oz capers
1 oz pine nuts
2 oz oil

Brown pine nuts in oil. Add stoned olives, chopped capers, origan and sauce Marinara. Heat to boiling for 3 minutes. Serve with spaghetti or linguini.

TUNA FISH
SAUCE
VILLAGGIO PACE

To serve 12 persons

1/2 lb onions
4 1/2 oz celery
5 1/2 oz olive oil
2 lbs ripe tomatoes
4 1/2 oz mushrooms
1/2 teaspoon origan
5 1/2 oz green olives
1 lb plain tuna fish or in olive
oil
3 oz tomato paste
salt as desired
1 teaspoon pepper
1/2 teaspoon sugar

Dip ripe tomatoes in boiling water for 2 minutes and rinse under cold running water to peel them easily. Remove seeds and chop. Finely chop celery and onions. Clean mushrooms and cut them into slices. Remove stones from olives and cut them into thin slices.
Heat oil in a pan, add chopped onions and celery and slowly brown for 10 minutes. Add mushrooms and cook for 2 minutes.
Add chopped tomatoes and 5 minutes after, tomato paste. Cook 20 minutes longer then add shredded tuna fish and olives. Add salt, pepper and sugar. Simmer for a few minutes and serve with noodles especially on hot days.

71

CERTOSINA
SAUCE

To serve 12 persons

2 lbs shrimps
1/2 lb cooked peas, fresh or canned
1/2 lb mushrooms
2 oz onions
4 1/2 oz butter
1 lb basil flavored tomato pulp
(Recipe N. 63)
1 bay leaf
1 teaspoon salt
1 teaspoon pepper

Sauté chopped onions and bay leaf in butter. Add cleaned mushrooms cut into half inch cubes. Cook for a couple of minutes then add shrimps cut into half inch dice. Cook over high heat for 5 minutes then add salt and pepper. Add cooked peas and tomato sauce. Heat to boiling for 2 minutes longer and serve with noodles or rice.

SAUSAGE

IN

MEAT GRAVY

To serve 12 persons

1 lb sausages
3 oz butter
3 oz white wine
1 oz scallion or onion
1/2 lb meat gravy (Recipe N. 59)

Put sausage in a casserole and cover with cold water.
Heat to boiling and remove. Drain in strainer and rinse under cold water. Skin sausage and cut it into pieces. Melt butter in a saucepan and as it froths add sausage. Allow to brown for 5 minutes then add finely chopped scallion or onion. Stir for one minute and sprinkle with white wine. Cook until wine is completely evaporated and add meat gravy. Allow to boil for 2 minutes and serve.
Excellent for lasagnas, rice, corn meal and any kind of noodles.

WHITE MILK
SAUCE

To serve 6 persons

3 oz butter
4 tablespoons flour
1 pint milk
salt as desired
1 pinch pepper
1 pinch nutmeg

Melt butter in a pot, add flour and stir until blended and flour gets yellowish. Pour lukewarm preboiled milk. Beat with a whip until flour is well blended with milk then cook for half hour. Frequently stirring, to prevent the formation of lumps. Add salt, pepper and nutmeg.
A basis for other recipes.

FOAMY SAUCE

To serve 6 persons

1 egg white
3 egg yolks
2 oz butter
2 oz heavy cream
1 pinch white pepper
1 lemon
salt as desired

Method 1. Combine all ingredients except lemon in a small pot. Beat well with a flexible whip and place pot in bain-marie. Keep on whipping until mixture becomes foamy like an egg nog. Remove from the bain-marie and add lemon juice constantly whipping. Serve at once otherwise transfer sauce in a cool container and keep it in a lukewarm place.

Method 2. Quicker. Combine all ingredients, except butter and lemon in an electric mixer. Set mixer on the low speed. Melt butter separately and gradually pour it in mixer, then add lemon juice and switch mixer on faster speed for a couple of minutes until well blended.
Excellent with cooked vegetables such as asparagus, zucchini, broccoli, cauliflower etc. or with boiled fish. Combined with other sauces will make them more delicate.

NEW
SAUCE
FOR STEAKS
AND
ROAST - BEEF

To serve 6 persons

3 oz fresh basil leaves or 1 oz dried
1 oz garlic
1 oz grated Parmesan or Swiss cheese
1 pinch salt
1 teaspoon Worcestershire Sauce
1 pinch pepper
3 oz butter
1 lemon

Strip basil leaves from stalks, wash and squeeze them. Using dried basil, dip it in lukewarm water for 10 minutes and squeeze. Combine basil, salt, garlic and grated cheese in a mortar and pound with pestle until mixture becomes almost creamy. Alternatively use an electric mixer. Add Worcestershire Sauce, pepper, softened butter and lemon juice, stir with a spoon until well mixed.
Serve with broiled steaks or roast-beef to give a new appetizing flavor and taste.

BAKED
LASAGNAS
ITALO - AMERICAN

To serve 12 persons

2 lbs lasagnas, fresh or dried
5 1/2 oz butter
1 lb creamed cottage cheese or Ricotta
1 1/2 lb strained tomato sauce (Recipe N. 60)
1 1/2 lb meat sauce (Recipe N. 54)
1/2 lb Mozzarella cheese
2 egg yolks
salt as desired
1 teaspoon pepper
1 pinch cinnamon, powdered
5 1/2 oz beef, finely ground
5 1/2 oz pork, finely ground
7 oz grated Parmesan cheese

Heat to boiling plenty of water in a stockpot adding about 1 teaspoon salt per quart. Dip fresh lasagnas and allow to boil for 3 minutes. If dried lasagnas are used, cook them for 15 minutes. Drain in a colander and sprinkle with fresh water to cool then spread lasagnas on a napkin to dry.

Combine creamed cottage cheese, one pinch of salt, cinnamon and egg yolks in a bowl. Mix thoroughly until well blended. Scald tomato sauce and meat sauce separately. Combine ground meats and shape into small balls. Sauté meat balls in a pan with a teaspoon of butter. Cut Mozzarella into 1/2-inch dice.

Butter a timbale mold or pyrex casserole. Spread a layer of meat sauce and tomato sauce. Arrange a layer of lasagnas, one by one, to cover sauce underneath. Sprinkle with grated Parmesan then spread a layer of creamed cottage cheese mixture evening it with a spoon. Stud with Mozzarella and meat balls. Go over again beginning with sauce, then lasagnas, Parmesan, creamed cottage cheese, meat balls and Mozzarella until mold is filled and all ingredients have been used.

Top mold with a layer of creamed cottage cheese mixture, dust with Parmesan and dot with diced Mozzarella and butter curls.

Bake in moderate oven for 10 minutes or until surface is golden brown. For best results bake in bain-marie placing mold in a larger pan containing half inch of water.

FRESH LASAGNAS

2 lbs flour
5 eggs
1 pinch salt
1 tablespoon olive oil
5 1/2 oz water

Combine flour, eggs, salt, water and oil. Knead well until dough becomes satiny smooth. Wrap in a napkin and let stand for half hour. Roll out dough with a rolling pin as thin as possible then cut it into 4 inch squares.

FETTUCCINI ALFREDO'S

78

To serve 6 persons

1 1/2 lb egg fettuccini
2 oz butter
2 1/2 oz heavy cream
1/2 teaspoon pepper
2 oz cooked ham
4 1/2 oz chicken meat, boiled
2 oz Grated Parmesan cheese

Cut ham and boiled chicken meat into thin strips.

Brown butter in a saucepan and add ham and chicken.

Brown slowly for a few minutes then add fettuccini previously cooked in 2 1/2 quarts salted water and well drained.

Delicately stir for a few minutes and pour heavy cream, sprinke with pepper and 1 oz grated Parmesan. Fold in very delicately and serve at once dusting each serving with remaining Parmesan.

MUSHROOM
PUDDING
APPIA ANTICA

To serve 12 persons
5 1/2 oz butter
1 lb fresh or canned mushrooms
salt as desired
1 teaspoon pepper
1 pinch nutmeg
4 1/2 oz flour
1 pint milk
3 oz grated cheese
4 egg yolks
1/2 lb meat gravy (Recipe N. 59)

Melt 3 1/2 oz butter in a small pot add flour and stir until well blended and yellowish. Pour lukewarm preboiled milk and blend in with a whip. Add salt, pepper and nutmeg and cook 20 minutes then allow to cool. Slightly brown remaining butter in a saucepan then add washed and chopped mushrooms, a pinch of salt and simmer until water is evaporated.

Combine prepared cream in a bowl with egg yolks adding them one by one constantly stirring, fold in mushrooms, grated cheese and salt. Butter individual molds and dredge with flour.

Pour mixture in molds to the level of half inch from rim.

Bake preferably in bain-marie for half hour. Unmold and serve coating with meat sauce.

MACARONI
TIMBALE
GIARDINO
DI CARPANETO

To serve 12 persons

2 oz butter
11 oz bread crumbs
1 pint White Milk Sauce
(Recipe N. 74)
1 1/2 pint Sauce Finanziera
(Recipe N. 58)
1 oz salt
1 pinch allspice
2 eggs
2 lbs small macaroni
grated cheese

Butter one or more timbale molds. For best results use three 4-serving molds. Repeatedly sprinkle with bread crumbs in such a way as to form a layer. Cook macaroni in 4 quarts salted water for 15 minutes. Drain and season with white milk and Finanziera sauces in equal amounts. Beat eggs with spices and fold in with macaroni. Fill molds, sprinkle surface with bread crumbs and dot with butter. Bake in moderate oven for 15 minutes.

Allow to cool then unmold coating with remaining Sauce Finanziera or serve it separately. Sprinkle each serving with grated cheese.

PORTOFINO
BAY RISOTTO

To serve 6 persons

4 1/2 oz butter
2 oz oil
1 lb shelled diced shrimps
1/2 lb fresh or canned tomatoes
5 1/2 oz peas
1 glass dry white wine
salt as desired
1 teaspoon black pepper
1/2 oz onion
1 lb rice
3 pints fish broth or other stocks
1 clove garlic
1 pinch sugar

Heat oil and 1 1/2 oz butter in a casserole and add finely chopped garlic, brown for 1 minute then add shrimps.

Allow to brown for 3 minutes and add chopped tomatoes, peas, salt, pepper and sugar. Cook for 10 minutes.

Melt 1 oz butter in a casserole and add chopped onion.

Allow to brown until transparent and add rice. Stir for a few minutes, sprinkle with wine and let evaporate.

Add boiling broth and continue cooking over high heat frequently stirring for 20 minutes. Take from heat and season with 3/4 shrimps sauce and remaining butter. Fold in well and serve, topping with remaining sauce.

Dust with grated cheese if desired.

CANNELLONI
CAPRI STYLE

To serve 6 persons

2 oz butter
1 lb creamed cottage cheese or
Ricotta
1 pinch nutmeg
1 pinch pepper
salt as desired
4 eggs
3 oz Mozzarella cheese
3 oz grated cheese
1/2 lb Basil flavored tomato
pulp (Recipe N. 63)
11 oz flour

Filling: Combine creamed cottage cheese, half grated cheese, a pinch of salt, pepper, nutmeg and 2 eggs in a bowl. Throughly mix until well blended.
Cannelloni: Make a dough combining flour, 2 eggs and a little water. Knead well until satiny smooth. Wrap in a napkin and let stand for half hour. Roll our paper thin and cut into 3 inch squares. Boil in salted water for 4 minutes dropping squares few at a time so that they won't stick together. Drain and sprinkle with fresh water then arrange on a napkin previously soaked in cold water and wrung.
Split filling on squares and roll them. Butter six individual au-gratin-dishes and spread a layer of tomato pulp on bottom. Arrange four cannelloni on each dish, coat with remaining tomato pulp, top with diced mozzarella, grated cheese and melted butter. 15 minutes before serving bake in moderate oven, preferably in bain-marie until slightly au gratin. Garnish with a few leaves of fresh basil.

LASAGNAS
A LA MODE
DU CHEF

To serve 12 persons

2 1/2 lbs fresh or dried lasagnas
1 lb Sauce Cacciatora (Recipe N. 55)

Basil sauce
10 1/2 oz fresh basil leaves or
2 oz dried basil
1 pinch salt
1 oz garlic
1 oz pine nuts
4 1/2 oz grated Parmesan cheese
2 oz grated piquant cheese
3 oz olive oil
1 pinch black pepper

Basil sauce: Wash, clean fresh basil and squeeze it dry.
Using dried basil, soak it in lukewarm water for half hour then drain and squeeze it. Combine basil, salt, garlic, pepper pine nuts 2 oz grated Parmesan and 2 oz piquant cheese.
Force all ingredients through food chopper twice or use an electric mixer until well blended, Blend in oil and two tablespoons water from cooking lasagnas.
Cook lasagnas in 4 quarts water and 1 oz salt. Cooking time varies according to the individual taste and the quality of lasagnas, 10 to 20 minutes. Drain and reserve water for basil sauce.
Divide lasagnas into two equal amounts and season half with basil sauce and half with Sauce Cacciatora.
Arrange on serving platter and serve. Besides the contrast in taste, the platter will look fine in its display; white lasagnas, red Sauce Cacciatora and green basil sauce. Sprinkle each portion with remaining Parmesan.

AGNOLOTTI
SOMBRERO

To serve 12 persons

1 recipe Ravioli filling (Recipe
N. 97)
1 recipe Ravioli dough (Recipe
N. 97)
2 eggs
1/2 lb heavy cream
1 lb meat gravy (Recipe N. 59)
4 1/2 oz Parmesan cheese
2 oz butter

Prepare ravioli dough, roll out very thin and cut it into 2
inch squares arranging them on a soaked napkin.
Stiffly beat eggs and brush square edges. Put 1 teaspoon
filling in center of each square and fold to shape a triangle.
Press two vertexes together until they stick so as to make a
kind of Mexican hat.
Cook agnolotti in salted water for 5 minutes and drain in a
colander.
Brown butter in a casserole and add well drained agnolotti,
gently sauté for 2 minutes then add heavy cream and meat
gravy.
Simmer for 10 minutes over very low heat until sauce is
smooth. Serve at once with a generous sprinkle of grated
Parmesan.

DELICIOUS
FOUR CHEESES
FETTUCCINI

To serve 12 persons

3 oz Swiss cheese, diced
3 oz Dutch cheese, diced
3 oz Fontina, diced
3 oz Parmesan, grated
4 1/2 oz butter
3 oz meat gravy (Recipe N. 59)
2 lbs fettuccini
4 quarts water
1 oz salt

Cook fettuccini as usual in salted water. Butter a shallow and broad casserole.
Arrange cooked fettuccini previously seasoned with 3 oz butter. Sprinkle with grated Parmesan, make a second layer with diced Swiss cheese, a third layer with diced Dutch cheese, top with Fontina and dot with remaining butter.
Bake in moderate oven until all cheeses melt through fettuccini. Take from oven and pour meat gravy. Serve at once.
The choice of cheeses varies depending on the individual tastes and availability on market.

SPAGHETTI PIE CAPRICCIO PARTENOPEO

To serve 12 persons

2 lbs spaghetti
6 eggs
5 1/2 oz butter
1 lb mushrooms
1/2 lb roast or boiled chicken
4 1/2 oz grated Parmesan cheese
salt as desired
1 teaspoon pepper
1 pinch nutmeg
1 clove garlic
1 oz parsley
4 1/2 oz heavy cream

Melt half butter with squeezed garlic, allow to brown for a few minutes, remove garlic and add mushrooms cut into thin slices, salt, pepper and finely chopped parsley.
Cook for 5 minutes and add chicken cut into small pieces.
Allow it to gain flavor, remove from heat and reserve.
Beat eggs and combine them with Parmesan and nutmeg.
Heat salted water to boiling and drop in spaghetti. Cook for 15 minutes. Drain and return to the pot and season with 2 oz butter. Add mushrooms and chicken mixture, fold in cream and beaten eggs until well blended. Add a little milk if overthickened.
Butter a baking dish and arrange spaghetti evening surface with a spoon. Sprinkle with grated Parmesan and dot with butter. Bake in moderate oven until au gratin.

CARMEN
RAREBITS

To serve 12 persons

48 bread slices, thin
24 ham slices, thin
24 Swiss cheese slices, thin
72 fresh mushrooms slices or
white truffles
1 pint milk
6 eggs
Oil for frying
1 lb meat gravy (Recipe N. 59)
2 glasses Port wine
1 teaspoon pepper
Savora mustard
Dredging flour

Cut away end crusts from bread slices. Spread them with
mustard and arrange one ham slice then white truffles or
mushrooms, dust with pepper, arrange one Swiss cheese
slice and cover with another bread slice sandwich like. Press
slightly and dip in cold milk. Squeeze away excess milk and
dredge with flour. Dip in stiffly beaten eggs and fry in hot
oil until golden brown.
Arrange on a plate with napkin and garnish with a tuft of
fresh parsley. Serve with meat gravy flavored with 2 glasses
of Port wine.

HAM
AND TOMATO
FETTUCCINI
ROMAN STYLE

To serve 6 persons

2 lbs egg fettuccini
4 1/2 oz ham
1/2 lb basil flavored tomato pulp
3 oz grated Parmesan cheese
2 oz butter
1 sprig sage

Brown butter with sage in a saucepan. Remove sage and add ham cut into strips wide as fettuccini. Slightly brown ham and add precooked fettuccini. Fold in delicately for a few minutes. Sprinkle with half of grated Parmesan then fold in tomato pulp. Serve at once with remaining Parmesan.
Cook fettuccini in salted boiling water frequently stirring for 10 to 20 minutes depending on tastes and quality.

BAKED
RICE
ANTILLAN
STYLE

To serve 12 persons

2 lbs rice
1/2 lb lean pork meat, diced
1/2 lb veal meat, diced
1/2 lb sliced sausage
48 littleneck clams
4 1/2 oz cooked peas
1/2 lb ripe tomatoes, coarsely chopped
1/2 lb red peppers, finely sliced
2 cloves garlic, chopped
2 oz onions, chopped
1 pinch powdered saffron
1/2 lb oil
2 1/2 quarts broth or water
salt as desired
1 lb medium sized shrimps, shelled
1 bay leaf
1 pinch of sugar

Combine 5 1/2 oz oil, haf onions, garlic, pork and veal meats in a casserole. Heat constantly stirring until meats begin to brown. Add tomatoes, a pinch of salt, sugar cover and simmer for 20 minutes. Add peppers, shrimps, sausage, bay leaf, cover and continue cooking for 10 minutes longer over low heat.

Sauté remaining onions in remaining oil in a broad saucepan without browning. Add rice and let it gain flavor for 2 minutes. Add prepared sauce, saffron, clams, peas and a pinch of salt. Pour broth or water. Heat to boiling then cover and place in oven for 20 minutes. Take from oven and let stand covered for 10 minutes and serve.

ARTICHOKE

PIE ZENA

To serve 6 persons

12 artichokes
1/2 lb creamed cottage cheese
or ricotta
2 oz grated Parmesan
1 teaspoon marjoram
4 eggs

4 tablespoons olive oil
2 oz butter
salt as desired
1 pinch pepper
1 clove of garlic
1 lemon
1/2 lb flour
water as necessary

Dough: Prepare a dough combining flour, a pinch of salt, 2 tablespoons oil and enough water to obtain a soft dough.
Knead well until satiny smooth. Wrap in a napkin and let stand for half hour.
Filling: Wash artichokes and remove outer leaves. Clip off woody parts outside and inside. Cut into halves lengthwise and then into strips. Sprinkle with the juice of one lemon and stir well.
Heat 2 oz butter and 2 tablespoons oil in a pan add artichokes a little salt and pepper, cover and simmer until tender over very low heat so as artichokes can stew without browning. Occasionally add a little water if stock dries too much. Remove and allow to cool.
Combine cooled off artichokes with creamed cottage cheese, eggs, grated cheese and finely chopped garlic and marjoram.
Mix until blended.
Split dough into 10 balls large as a walnut. Roll out each ball very thin and as round as possible.
Oil a round baking pan and arrange a sheet of dough oiling it with a brush. Repeat the operation for six times always brushing each sheet with oil.
Pour filling and even it. Lay remaining sheets of dough following the same procedure. Fold excess dough towards center of pan and press it on rim like a pastry shell.
Oil surface and bake in moderate oven for half hour. Brush surface every 5 minutes with oil.
Serve hot, lukewarm or cold.

CHAMPAGNE RISOTTO

To serve 6 persons

1 lb rice
2 oz butter
4 1/2 oz cream cheese
1 oz onion
1/2 bottle dry Champagne
1 pint veal or chicken broth
1 pinch white pepper
salt as desired

Chop onion, put in a strainer and freely sprinkle with fresh water. Drain and squeeze it inside a napkin so that it looses its strenght. Heat butter in a casserole, add onion and sauté over low heat without browning.
Add rice and stir for 3 minutes then pour boiling broth.
Increase heat and cook for 10 minutes frequently stirring. As soon as broth is evaporated add Champagne gradually while cooking for another 20 minutes. Add pepper, cream cheese and stir well. Serve at once.

LASAGNAS AU GRATIN TAORMINA FASHION

To serve 12 persons

2 lbs lasagnas
1/2 lb Mozzarella or Swiss cheese
5 1/2 oz grated Parmesan cheese
1 1/2 lb basil flavored tomato pulp
2 1/2 lbs eggplants
6 1/2 oz oil
1/2 pint milk, dairy fresh
Dredging flour
2 oz butter

Cut peeled eggplants into half inch slices. Add a little salt and dip them in milk. Squeeze and dredge with flour.
Fry in hot oil on both sides until golden brown. Drain on a grate to remove excess oil.
Cook lasagnas as described in Recipe N. 77. Scald tomato pulp. Oil a saucepan, preferably pyrexware. Spread on bottom a thin layer of tomato pulp. Arrange a layer of eggplants and then a layer of lasagnas. Sprinkle with grated Parmesan. Go on with another layer of eggplants, sprinkle with grated Parmesan, tomato sauce, diced Mozzarella or Swiss cheese, lasagnas. Fill baking pan up to 1/2 inch from rim repeating the same operation. Top with a layer of eggplants, diced cheese grated cheese, tomato pulp and dot with butter. Bake in moderate oven for 10 to 15 minutes or until au gratin.

RAVIOLI

SAN VITO

To serve 12 persons

2 lbs flour
Water
3 tablespoons oil
salt
2 lbs beets
1 lb creamed cottage cheese or ricotta
1/2 lb sausage
1 lb sweetbreads and brains

4 1/2 oz grated cheese
6 eggs
2 oz onions
2 cloves garlic
3 1/2 oz butter
1 teaspoon pepper
1 pinch nutmeg
1 lb Sauce Finanziera (Recipe N. 58)

Dough: Combine flour, 1 tablespoon oil, salt and water. Knead for 5 minutes or until satiny smooth. Wrap in a napkin and let stand for half hour.

Filling: Cook beets in water, drain and squeeze excess water. Clean sweetbreads and brains and allow to boil for 5 minutes. Take from heat and leave in stock for 10 minutes then drain.
Sauté chopped onions and squeezed garlic in a saucepan with 2 tablespoons oil and 1 oz butter. Add sausage, sweetbreads and brains and sauté for a few minutes. Remove garlic and add coarsely chopped beets. Allow to gain flavor for a while mixing all ingredients. Force through food chopper using coarse attachment. Combine in a bowl with four eggs, grated cheese, nutmeg, salt and pepper.
Mix until well blended.
Roll out dough as thin as possible and cut into 3-inch wide strips preferably with pastry wheel. Brush strips with remaining stiffly beaten eggs and arrange 1 teaspoon filling in the lower part of strip every 1 inch until it is filled. Fold empty half of strip on filling and slightly press edges and gaps to seal. Cut ravioli with a pastry wheel so as to form little "pillows".
Cook ravioli in 4 quarts water and 1 oz salt for not longer than 5 minutes. Delicately drain in a large colander and season with remaining melted butter and hot Sauce Finanziera. Sprinkle with grated Parmesan if desired.

COUNTRYSIDE GOLDEN FETTUCCINI

To serve 12 persons

2 1/2 lbs fettuccini
5 1/2 oz butter
5 1/2 oz boiled peas
1/2 lb chicken livers
1 lb mushrooms, fresh or canned
1/2 lb sausage
5 1/2 oz Swiss cheese
2 oz onions
1 pinch pepper
salt as desired
Meat gravy (optional)

Cook fettuccini as usual in 5 quarts boiling water with 1 1/2 oz salt.

Sauté chopped onions in a saucepan with 2 oz butter until brown. Add mushrooms cut into thin slices and cook for 5 mintues then add cooked peas and stir for a few minutes.

Add one pinch of salt and pepper and take from heat.

Sauté peeled and sliced sausage in another pan until slightly brown. Add diced chicken livers previously cleaned and washed. Cook for 5 minutes over high heat and pour into peas and mushrooms mixture. Butter one or more baking casseroles preferably pyrexware. Season fettuccini with prepared mixture and transfer in baking casserole. Even surface with a spoon, spread diced Swiss cheese and dot with remaining butter.

Bake in oven until golden. A little meat gravy spread on surface before baking will enhance flavor.

Serve at once.

POTATO
DUMPLINGS
OLD
TURIN

To serve 6 persons

4 lbs potatoes
1 lb flour
1 pinch nutmeg
2 eggs
1 pinch pepper
salt as desired
4 1/2 oz Fontina or other
soft rennet cheese
1 lb Meat sauce with
mushrooms (Recipe N. 57)

Pare potatoes and wash thoroughly. Allow to boil whole for half hour in salted water. Drain well then force through potato ricer. Arrange on a board and combine with 14 oz flour. Beat eggs with pepper and nutmeg and add to potatoes and flour kneading well until blended.
Split potato dough into ten pieces. Roll in dough on floured board to make long dredged strips about 3/4 inch in diameter. Cut strips with a knife into 3/4 inch long bits. Dredge with more flour if too moist but consider that excessive flour makes heavy dumplings.
Hold a fork in left hand with prongs steadily touching board. Take a bit each time and press it against prongs to make a kind of slot in dumpling.
Drop dumplings into 4 quarts boiling water with 1 1/2 oz salt gradually. Stir delicately while cooking. When dumplings come to the surface remove with skimmer and put in a shallow and broad baking casserole so that dumplings won't stick together. Season with meat sauce with mushrooms folding in carefully and add diced cheese. Bake in oven for 2 minutes or until cheese melts through dumplings. Serve at once. To vary, season with meat sauce (Recipe N. 54) or with basil flavored tomato pulp (Recipe n. 63).

CHEESE SOUFFLE' EMMENTAL VALLEY

To serve 12 persons

2 1/2 oz Cornstarch
2 1/2 oz flour
1 pint milk
5 1/2 oz butter
12 eggs, separated
12 oz diced Swiss cheese
1 pinch nutmeg
1 pinch pepper
1 pinch salt

Combine butter, cornstarch and flour, knead and shape into a ball. Heat milk to boiling adding salt, pepper and nutmeg. Drop prepared ball and stir until mixture becomes smooth for about 3 minutes. When mixture becomes thick enough and detaches from pot, remove from heat and cool to lukewarm. Add egg yolks one by one constantly stirring and then add diced Swiss cheese. Stiffly beat egg whites with 1 pinch salt and a few drops of lemon juice and fold in mixture.
Butter individual remekins or molds and dredge with flour. Fill with prepared mixture 1 inch from rim and bake in moderate oven for 15 minutes about.
Serve at once.

FETTUCCINI OCEANIC SPECIAL

To serve 12 persons

2 1/2 lbs egg fettuccini
4 1/2 oz butter
5 1/2 oz heavy cream
1 teaspoon freshly ground black pepper
4 1/2 oz boiled ham
1/2 lb chicken or turkey, boiled or roast
4 1/2 oz grated cheese
2 tablespoons Cognac or Brandy

Cut chicken and ham into thin strips. Brown butter in a saucepan and add chicken and ham. Sauté for a few minutes then sprinkle with Cognac. If the pan is on a gas range, tilt pan over flame so that Cognac will ignite, or use a match. Allow blazing to continue until Cognac is burnt aut. Add well drained fettuccini previously cooked in 4 quarts water and 1 1/2 oz salt. Sauté for a few minutes and fold in cream. Sprinkle with pepper and half grated cheese.
Stir and serve with remaining grated cheese.

GREEN LASAGNAS AU GRATIN GASTRONOMIC

To serve 12 persons
2 1/2 lbs flour
3 oz spinach purée
6 eggs
salt as desired
5 1/2 oz butter
2 pints milk
1/2 lb grated cheese
2 lbs meat sauce (Recipe N. 54)
1 pinch nutmeg

Green Lasagnas: Combine 2 lbs flour, spinach purée, a pinch of salt and eggs. Knead well until smooth and let stand for half hour covered. Roll out thin and cut into 3-inch squares.

Cream sauce: Melt 3 oz butter in a small pot, add 3 oz flour and stir until flour becomes yellowish. Pour boiled milk and whip thoroughly until well blended and smooth, add a pinch of salt and nutmeg and simmer for 20 minutes over low heat.

Cook lasagnas into 4 quarts boiling water and 1 1/2 oz salt. Use a broad pot so that lasagnas won't stick together. Cook for not longer than 5 minutes. Drain and sprinkle with fresh water to cool then spread on a napkin.

Butter one or more baking pans and spread a little cream sauce on bottom then arrange a first layer of lasagnas.

Spread a layer of meat sauce and sprinkle with grated cheese. Continue arranging lasagnas, meat sauce, cream sauce and grated cheese up to half inch from rim. Top with a last layer of lasagnas and spread remaining cream sauce. Sprinkle with grated cheese and dot with butter.

Bake in moderate oven for 20 minutes until au gratin.

EGGS WITH CLAMS FISHERMAN'S STYLE

To serve 3 persons

6 eggs
1 lb live clams or 4 1/2 oz canned
2 oz oil
1 clove garlic
2 ripe tomatoes
salt as desired
1 pinch pepper
1 oz parsley

Peel tomatoes, squeeze out seeds and chop finely. Chop parsley and garlic. Heat live clams in pan with one tablespoon oil until open. Take from range and remove shells.

Strain clam liquor through cheesecloth or napkin without shaking pan so that any sand remains on bottom. Sauté oil and garlic in a saucepan then add tomatoes and strained clam liquor. Cook over high heat until reduced add a pinch of salt and pepper and fold in clams. Take from heat to prevent clams from cooking. Spread an equal amount of sauce into three individual casseroles. Heat and break eggs over sauce, two each serving. Sprinkle with chopped parsley and cook for 2 minutes. Serve at once.

Using canned clams just follow the same procedure.

POACHED
EGGS
WITH
CORNED BEEF

To serve 3 persons

6 eggs
3 tablespoons white vinegar
salt as desired
1/2 lb corned beef
1/2 lb boiled potatoes
2 oz butter

Dice potatoes and corned beef and sauté together in butter stirring constantly. Remove and split on three plates.
Pour enough water in a broad casserole to cover a standing egg, add vinegar and heat to simmering without adding salt. Break eggs one by one and slip them into water. Simmer for about 2 minutes or until white is firm. Remove with skimmer, drain and serve on sautéed potatoes and corned beef.
Wishing to prepare eggs ahead of time, precook as outlined above and just before serving dip poached eggs in salted boiling water for one minute, drain on a napkin and serve.

POACHED
EGGS
BENEDICT

To serve 3 persons

6 poached eggs (Recipe N. 104)
6 slices boiled ham
6 toasts
6 tablespoons Foamy Sauce (Recipe N. 75)
1 oz butter

Trim toasts a little larger than an egg. Sauté ham slices in butter very slightly. Arrange a slice of ham on each toast and top with poached egg. Coat with Foamy Sauce.
As a change, use smoked salmon instead of ham.
Serve with buttered asparagus tips garnished with a thin slice of black truffle or a buttered mushroom cap.

FLAT LETTUCE OMELET SANTA MARGHERITA

To serve 3 persons

3 lettuce hearts
6 eggs
1 oz grated cheese
1 clove garlic
1 pinch marjoram
1 pinch pepper
1 pinch salt
2 oz olive oil
3 toasts
1 glass cold milk

Sauté chopped garlic in skillet with 1 oz oil and add lettuce cut into thin strips. Cover and cook until braised and dry.
Trim crust from toasts and soak them in cold milk for 5 minutes. Gently squeeze away excess milk and chop. Mince marjoram and combine with grated cheese. Break eggs in a bowl add salt, pepper and grated cheese mixture and stir. Add lettuce and chopped bread constantly stirring until well blended. Heat remaining oil in a frypan and pour prepared mixture. Cook over moderate heat until eggs are set.
Place a plate on omelet and holding it steadily but gently turn frypan upside down so that omelet falls on plate.
Oil again frypan if necessary, slip omelet and continue cooking on other side until well firm.
To vary, try it with any other vegetable such as artichokes, spinach, beets, etc.

SCRAMBLED EGGS WITH MUSHROOMS

To serve 3 persons

6 eggs
1/2 lb mushrooms
2 oz butter
2 oz parsley
1/2 lemon
1 pinch salt
1 pinch pepper
1 clove garlic

Thoroughly clean mushrooms and cut into thin slices.
Finely chop parsley leaves. Melt butter in pan with whole
squeezed garlic, add mushrooms and juice of half lemon.
Stir well, add salt and pepper and allow to cook over high
heat for 5 minutes. Remove garlic and add slightly beaten
eggs and parsley. Stir with a fork until eggs are nearly firm.
Serve at once with toasts.

SPANISH FLAT OMELET

To serve 3 persons

1 small onion
2 peppers
2 ripe tomatoes
1 oz parsley
salt as desired
2 oz oil or butter
1 pinch sugar

Cut onion into thin slices. Wash peppers, remove seeds and cut into strips. Peel tomatoes, remove seeds and chop coarsely. Finely chop parsley leaves.
Heat oil in a pan add onion and sauté for 5 minutes without browning. Add peppers and sauté 5 minutes longer. Add tomatoes, a pinch of salt and sugar. Cook until water is evaporated and sauce is almost reduced. Slightly beat eggs with a pinch of salt. Pour 3/4 of prepared sauce.
Mix and make an omelet as described in Recipe N. 106.
Cover with remaining sauce and chopped parsley.

SHIRRED EGGS WITH CHICKEN LIVERS PRINCIPESSA

To serve 3 persons

6 eggs
6 chicken livers
24 asparagus tips
2 oz butter
1 pinch salt
1 pinch pepper
1 sage leaf

Accurately clean and wash chicken livers and cut into four pieces. Cut previously steamed asparagus tips into 1 inch pieces. Melt butter in a skillet and add sage leaf and chicken livers. Sauté for 2 minutes then stir and continue cooking over high heat for 5 minutes or until golden brown. Remove sage leaf and add asparagus tips, sprinkle with salt and pepper and cook for 2 minutes longer.
Serve with shirred eggs.
Melt 1 teaspoon butter in individual skillets or suitable metal or pyrex shirred egg dishes. Allow butter to become golden brown and break eggs in. Cook to the desired firmness and sprinkle salt over whites and not over yolks.

WESTERN
OMELET

To serve 3 persons

6 eggs
1 small onion
2 ripe tomatoes
2 peppers
2 oz boiled ham
2 oz bacon strips
1 oz butter

Cut bacon into thin strips and put in pan. Heat and as soon as fat begins to melt add finely sliced onion.
Sauté for 5 minutes frequently stirring. Add diced tomatoes and peppers and cook until sauce is thickened. Take from heat. Slightly beat eggs with a pinch of salt in a bowl and fold in prepared sauce.
Melt butter in a frypan and add ham cut into thin strips.
Sauté for 2 minutes and pour egg mixture. Hold frypan handle and shake it with short but fast strokes until eggs are firm but not hard. Let pan stand for a while so as a thin crust can form under omelet. Loosen edges of omelet with a fork and fold it to shape a half-moon. Carefully loosen other half and slip omelet onto a plate.

TILLERS' OMELET

To serve 3 persons

6 eggs ·
1 medium sized potato
1 small zucchini
4 1/2 oz celery hearts
4 1/2 oz spinach
1 ripe tomato
2 oz oil
Salt and pepper as desired

Wash and peel all vegetables. Dice and keep separated.
Heat oil in a pan and add potato and celery. Delicately stir
for 5 minutes and add zucchini. 5 minutes thereafter add
spinach and tomato, salt and pepper. Stir for a few minutes
longer and take from heat. Slightly beat eggs in a bowl and
fold in prepared vegetables. Make a flat omelet as outlined
in Recipe N. 106.

HARD
BOILED
EGGS
A LA KING

To serve 3 persons

6 eggs
3 oz boiled peas
3 oz mushrooms
2 red pepeprs, roasted
1/2 lb White Milk Sauce
(Recipe N. 74)
1 glass Sherry wine
1 glass Yoghourt or sour
cream
1 oz butter
salt as desired

Cover eggs with boiling water and cook for 7 minutes. Cool and remove shells. Cut eggs into halves lenghtwise and reserve on a plate.
Clean mushrooms, cut into four pieces and sauté in a frying pan with butter for 5 minutes, then add peppers cut into thin strips, peas and salt and cook for a few minutes longer.
Heat White Milk Sauce to boiling. Remove from heat and blend in yoghourt or sour cream. Fold in Sherry and prepared mixture.
Arrange egg halves onto three individual casseroles and cover with sauce. Scald and serve at once with toasts.

EGGS
FINE
SICILIAN

To serve 3 persons

6 eggs
2 oz olive oil
1 clove garlic
1 pinch origan
1 tablespoon tomato extract
2 eggplants, medium sized
1 pinch pepper
1 pinch sugar
salt as desired

Peel eggplants and cut them into 1 inch cubes. Sprinkle with salt and squeeze excess water away. Heat oil in a frying pan and add squeezed garlic and eggplants. Sauté for 5 minutes then add tomato extract, origan, sugar and peper. Cook 5 minutes longer, remove garlic and split mixture into three individual casseroles. Break in eggs and cook until set. Serve at once.

HAM
AND EGGS
WITH
SWISS
CHEESE

To serve 3 persons

6 eggs
3 boiled ham slices
3 Swiss Cheese slices
2 oz butter

Brown butter into three individual casseroles, preferably pyrexware. Add ham slices and sauté for 2 minutes on both sides. Break two eggs in each casserole and cover with cheese slices. Bake in moderate oven until cheese melts through eggs. Serve at once.

To serve 3 persons

6 eggs
1/2 glass water
4 1/2 oz onions
4 1/2 oz boneless chicken meat, boiled or roast
2 oz bean sprouts, canned
2 oz water chestnuts
1/2 teaspoon vegetable extract
Salt and pepper as desired
3 teaspoon Soy sauce
3 oz butter
5 1/2 oz rice
1 tablespoon cornstarch
1 pinch sugar

THICK OMELET LOTUS FLOWER

Cut onions into very thin slices. Dice chicken. Drain canned bean sprouts and reserve water. Cut chestnuts into thin slices. Boil or bake rice for 25 minutes and keep it covered in a warm place. Sauté onions in pan with 2 oz oil or butter for 5 minutes, add chicken, bean sprouts, chestnuts a pinch of salt and pepper. Stir over heat for 3 minutes longer and remove.

Combine eggs in a bowl with water, a pinch of salt and 1 teaspoon soy sauce. Mix well and fold in prepared mixture.

Oil a skillet and prepare three flat omelets following directions of Recipe N. 106. Omelets must be small in size but thick so choose a rather small skillet in proportion to the amount of mixture to be cooked.

Heat one glass water to boiling adding a pinch of sugar.

Blend cornstarch in reserved bean sprouts water and add to boiling water. Blend in remaining butter, vegetable extract and 2 teaspoons soy sauce. Cook for 2 minutes.

Season rice with prepared sauce and serve with omelet.

Being some of the used ingredients not always easily available in trade, replace bean sprouts with tender celery hearts, chestnuts with mushrooms and soy sauce with a good liquid beef extract.

To vary use shrimps or lobster or pork meat instead of chicken.

115

SHRIMPS
IN SKEWER
BARONESS
MIRIAN

To serve 6 persons

30 Jumbo shrimps
18 mushrooms
2 lbs potatoes
salt as desired
1 teaspoon freshly ground pepper
3 tablespoons Brandy or

Cognac
6 bay leaves
6 green and red peppers
1 pinch origan
3 oz oil
3 oz butter
1 clove garlic
1 lemon

Thoroughly clean and wash shrimps. Remove shells and pat them dry with a napkin. Marinate for half hour with brandy a pinch of salt, pepper and bay leaves. Roast peppers and sprinkle with cold water to remove skins. Cut into halves and remove seeds. Place in a covered pan with oil, sprinkle with origan and keep warm. Clean mushrooms. Remove stems to be cut into dice and reserve whole caps. Wash and pare potatoes and cut them into half inch cubes.
Heat 2 oz oil and 1 oz butter in a pan adding squeezed garlic.
Drop potatoes and mushrooms stems.
Stir frequently with a spatula and allow to cook for 10 to 15 minutes. Remove from heat and sprinkle with salt. Keep warm.
Fill six skewers in the following order: one shrimps, one mushrooms cap, one shrimp, one bay leaf. Continue until there are 5 shrimps and 3 mushrooms caps on each skewer.
Melt remaining butter in a pan and cook skewers for 10 to 15 minutes basting with liquid in pan. Sprinkle salt and lemon juice and serve with prepared peppers and potatoes.

LOBSTER
SAPPHIRES
QUEEN
OF MAINE

To serve 6 to 12 persons

6 lbs lobster
2 oz scallion
1 oz garlic
1/2 oz tarragon leaves
1/2 oz chervil
1/2 oz parsley
3 bay leaves
4 lbs tomatoes, ripe
2 oz salt

1 1/2 teaspoon pepper
3 oz butter
3 oz olive oil
1 pinch Cayenne pepper or Tabasco
1 lb mushrooms
1 lb spinach noodles
1/2 pint dry white wine
6 tablespoons Cognac or Brandy

Cut live lobster tail into 1 inch pieces. Cut head into halves lenghtwise. Remove entrails reserving liver and coral if present.

Heat oil in a casserole, add lobster, salt and pepper.

As it begins to brown add 4 tablespoons brandy and let evaporate. Add chopped scallion and 2/3 squeezed garlic. Heat for 1 minute, stir and pour white wine. Let evaporate and then add peeled and chopped tomatoes and the "bouquet" made with 1/3 tarragon, parsley, chervil and bay leaves all tied together with a thin thread. Cover and allow to cook for half hour. If the sauce becomes too thick, gradually add a little water but keep covered.

When lobster is done, remove from casserole and shell.

Reserve lobster meat in a covered pan and keep warm.

Remove bouquet of herbs and press sauce through a sieve, cracking shells, head and claws as well. Pour strained sauce over lobster meat and heat to boiling for 1 minute. Take from heat, add chopped entrails, 1 oz butter, a pinch of Cayenne pepper, remaining chopped tarragon leaves, 2 tablespoons brandy and salt as desired.

Sauté sliced mushrooms in pan with remaining butter and squeezed garlic for a few minutes over high heat. Remove garlic and fold in lobster meat.

Serve with spinach noodles seasoned with a little butter.

STUFFED
SMELTS
KEY WEST

To serve 6 persons

26 smelts
1 lb bread crumbs
1/2 pint milk
6 eggs
2 oz grated cheese
1 teaspoon marjoram, chopped
2 cloves garlic, chopped
1 lb peas, boiled
2 lbs oil for frying
1 pinch pepper
1 oz onions

Cut away heads of smelts, Open lenghtwise and remove spines leaving tails. Wash thoroughly and spread on a plate to drain. Mince six smelts with a knife removing tails.

Combine chopped marjoram and garlic with grated cheese. Soak bread crumbs in milk for 10 minutes. Squeeze and chop it. Beat eggs in a bowl and combine grated cheese mixture, pepper, chopped crumbs and boiled peas.

Sauté chopped onions in a pan with 2 tablespoons oil until transparent, add minced smelts. Stir for 2 minutes still over heat and fold in egg mixture. Add salt as desired.

Heat oil for frying in a pan, fill smelts with 1 tablespoon stuffing and delicately slip them into hot oil. Allow to fry until golden brown for about 5 minutes. Remove with skimmer and drain on a grate.

Serve with lemon seasoned lettuce hearts.

PECONIC BAY SCALLOPS FLAVORED WITH RED LABEL WHISKY SAUCE

To serve 6 persons

1 1/2 lbs shelled scallops
1 pint milk
2 bay leaves
1 sprig thyme
3/4 oz scallion
1/2 lb mushrooms
1 sprig tarragon, chopped
1 tablespoon minced parsley
salt as desired
1 pinch Cayenne pepper
6 tablespoons Scotch Whisky
1/2 oz cornstarch or arrowroot
1 egg white
3 egg yolks
4 1/2 oz heavy cream
10 1/2 oz rice
4 1/2 oz butter

119

Combine scallops in a pan, with milk, a pinch of salt, thyme and bay leaves. Heat to boiling for 1 minute then remove scallops with a skimmer. Strain milk and reserve. Melt 3 oz butter in saucepan, add finely chopped scallion, parsley and tarragon leaves. As butter begins to froth add sliced mushrooms and 5 minutes after drop scallops. Stir gently and sprinkle cornstarch. Keep on stirring for another minute then add reserved milk. Cook for 5 minutes longer, remove from heat and place in bain-marie.

Combine egg white and yolks, heavy cream, whisky, Cayenne pepper in a bowl and beat until stiff. Cook for a few minutes over low heat constantly beating and pour over scallops. Stir and add more salt and pepper if desrired. Serve with boiled rice seasoned with melted butter.

SOLE
FILLETS
IN MARTINI DRY
VERMOUTH

To serve 6 persons

2 lbs sole fillets
1 oz scallion
3 oz butter
4 1/2 oz spinach
4 1/2 ripe tomatoes
salt as desired
1 pinch white pepper
1 teaspoon cornstarch
4 1/2 oz heavy cream
4 1/2 oz Dry Vermouth
2 egg yolks

Butter a saucepan, preferably pyrexware, spread half of chopped scallion on bottom and arrange sole fillets.
Sprinkle with a little salt and dot with butter. Pour 3 oz Dry Vermouth over fillets, cover and simmer for 10 minutes. Remove from heat and reserve in a lukewarm place covered.
Clean and wash spinach. Cut leaves only into thin strips.
Wash, peel and remove seeds from tomatoes then chop.
Sauté remaining chopped scallion with 1 oz butter then add spinach, tomatoes, a pinch of salt and pepper and allow to cook for 5 minutes. Sprinkle cornstarch stirring with a spoon, cook for 1 minute longer and pour heavy cream. Reduce heat and simmer for 5 minutes adding dripping from cooking fillets. Take from heat.
Beat egg yolks with remaining vermouth and fold in sauce constantly stirring. Add more salt if desired and remaining butter cut into small bits. Stir until well blended and pour sauce over fillets. Serve with toasts or puff pastes.

120

BROILED SWORD FISH STEAK

To serve 6 persons

2 1/2 lbs sword fish, six steaks
3 1/2 oz dry white wine
2 lemons
1 sprig thyme
3 bay leaves
1 oz onion
1 pinch salt
1 teaspoon pepper
3 oz oil
1 oz butter
1 oz parsley

Marinate sword fish steaks for one hour in a shallow porcelain bowl with white wine, lemon juice, thyme, bay leaves, finely chopped onion, salt and pepper.
Drain steaks from marinade and rub with oil. Broil like a common steak for 5 to 6 minutes on each side.
During cooking brush steaks every half minute with oil. Strain marinade and add finely chopped parsley leaves. Heat to boiling and add dots of butter.
Allow to boil one minute longer to blend in butter and serve on steaks with steamed potato salad seasoned with a little mayonnaise and rasped horseradish.

SUPREME
OF HADDOCK
CHARLOTTE
AMALIE

To serve 6 persons

2 1/2 lbs haddock fillets
3 1/2 oz milk
6 1/2 oz oil
2 oz butter
1 oz garlic
1/2 lb peppers
1/2 lb tomatoes, ripe
1 teaspoon black pepper
1 pinch sugar
salt as desired
Dredging flour

Dip haddock fillets into cold milk. Drain and dredge with flour. Heat 5 1/2 oz oil in a pan and fry fillets until golden brown. Remove and place in a casserole sprinkling with salt and freshly ground pepper as desired.
Wash and cut tomatoes and peppers into thin strips.
Heat butter and remaining oil in a pan and add finely sliced garlic. Sauté until brown then add tomatoes and peppers, a pinch of salt and sugar. Reduce heat and simmer for 10 minutes. Pour sauce over fillets and 10 minutes before serving place in hot oven.

CHILLED FRESH SALMON, CHAMPAGNE FLAVORED

To serve 6 persons

6 1/2-inch thick salmon steaks
3 oz olive oil
1/2 oz salt
1 teaspoon white pepper
4 lemons
1/2 bottle Dry Champagne
3 tablespoons Strained Tomato Sauce (Recipe N. 60)
1 teaspoon French mustard

Accurately clean salmon steaks and arrange in a saucepan preferably pyrexware. Sprinkle with oil, salt, pepper, juice of lemons and champagne. Cover and cook over moderate heat for 15 minutes. Drain salmon steaks and transfer in another saucepan. Combine dripping from cooking steaks in a bowl with remaining lemon juice, tomato sauce and mustard. If necessary add more salt and pepper, but be sure sauce does not get too thick. Coat salmon steaks with sauce and chill before serving. It can be stored in refrigerator for a few days.
Serve with a chilled cucumber salad flavored with finely chopped dill and pepper.

FLORIDA
POMPANO
A LA VIRA

To serve 6 persons

3 lbs pompano fillets
1 lb potatoes
1 lb zucchini
2 lbs oil for frying
Dredging flour
3 oz butter
1/2 oz salt
1 lemon
1 oz parsley

Cut pompano fillets into thin strips. Likewise cut potatoes
and zucchini previously pared. Heat oil in a pan. Dredge fish
and zucchini with flour and fry together with potatoes.
Drain well.
Heat butter in a pan and sauté fish, potatoes and zucchini.
Sprinkle with salt, lemon juice and finely chopped parsley.
Serve hot.
Use sole or other fillets instead of pompano.

ANNAMARIA STUFFED LOBSTER AU GRATIN

To serve 6 persons

3 lobsters, 2 lbs each
1/2 lb Alaska crab meat
4 1/2 oz butter
1 oz scallion
1/2 lb fresh mushrooms
3 oz dry white wine
1 lb White milk Sauce (Recipe N. 74)
2 egg yolks
1 teaspoon white pepper
1 oz parsley
salt as desired
2 oz grated cheese

Dip live lobsters in salted boiling water enough to cover them. Allow to boil for half hour. Drain and cool.
Cut lobsters into halves lenghtwise and remove meat without breaking shells. Dice lobster meat and reserve on a plate. Cut crab meat same as lobster and remove any bits of shell. Clean mushrooms and cut them into small cubes. Melt 3 oz butter in a saucepan and add mushrooms and chopped scallion. Sauté for 5 minutes and add lobster and crab meats. Delicately stir for 2 minutes then pour white wine. Let evaporate and add half of white milk sauce, chopped parsley, salt and pepper. Arrange lobster shells in a baking pan and fill with prepared mixture. Blend egg yolks with remaining White Milk Sauce and spread an even layer on filled lobster shells. Dust with grated cheese and pour remaining melted butter over cheese.
Bake in oven until golden brown. Garnish with tufts of parsley and uncork a bottle of Dry Champagne!

RED OR GRAY

SNAPPER

MISS LYNN

To serve 6 persons

4 lbs snapper
1 lb onions
2 oz parsley
1 oz garlic
1 pinch saffron
Fish stock
1/2 oz cornstarch or arrowroot
2 oz dry white wine
6 pepper grains
salt as desired
4 1/2 oz oil
1 oz butter

Make steaks or fillets with snapper. Put fins, backbones and heads into a saucepot and cover with 1 quart water or more, add pepper grains, salt, parsley stalks, reserving leaves and heat to boiling for half hour. Strain stock.
Heat oil in a large casserole and add sliced onions, chopped garlic and saffron. Cook over low heat for 15 minutes.
Stir for 2 minutes, pour white wine and allow to evaporate completely. Add strained fish stock. Increase heat to high and cook for 5 minutes then add fish. Cook for 10 minutes and take from heat. Transfer drained fish in another saucepan. Strain sauce through a sieve, pour over fish and heat to boiling. Blend cornstarch with softened butter and add to sauce. Cook for another 2 minutes and take from heat. Finely chop parsley leaves and sprinkle over fish adding more salt if desired. Serve with hot croutons or toasts.

SEA
BASS
OLD PORT
WAY

To serve 6 persons

2 lbs tomatoes
3 bay leaves
1 sprig thyme
2 teaspoons minced dill
1 oz garlic
1/2 lb black olives
6 sea bass steaks or 6 small
whole sea bass
5 1/2 oz oil
4 1/2 oz dry white wine
1 teaspoon pepper
salt as desired

Wash, peel and remove seeds from tomatoes then chop.
Remove olive stones and chop garlic.
Heat oil in a saucepan and add fish. Brown for 2 minutes on
each side. Pour white wine and allow to evaporate half of it.
Add a pinch of salt and pepper, chopped tomatoes, bay
leaves, dill, thyme and chopped garlic. Cover and cook over
low heat for 15 minutes then add olives and simmer for a
few minutes until olives are hot. Serve at once with steamed
potatoes and toasted croutons rubbed with garlic.

JUMBO SHRIMPS CURRY M.R.S.

Wash shrimps, clean and drain. Remove seeds from peppers, wash and cut into half inch dice. Chop mango and banana, combine in a bowl and sprinkle with lemon juice. Slice onions and sauté over low heat in butter until tender. Add shrimps and increase heat. Three minutes after add paprika and curry, sprinkle with salt and pour water to cover shrimps. Cook for 5 minutes, remove shrimps with skimmer and reserve in a covered bowl. Strain sauce through a sieve, return to saucepan and add peppers. Heat to boiling for 5 minutes then add mango and banana mixture and sprinkle with lime juice. Simmer 3 minutes longer and add shrimps. Reheat and serve with boiled rice.

To serve 6 persons

60 jumbo shrimps
5 1/2 oz butter
salt as desired
2 lemons
2 green peppers
1 teaspoon paprika
1 1/4 oz Curry powder
1 mango
6 1/2 oz onions
1 banana
3/4 lb rice
1 lime

FAVOURITE ROAST AND GLAZED STRIPED BASS OF NEAR EAST

To serve 6 persons

4 lbs striped bass
1 tablespoon flour
1 1/2 pint dry white wine
6 pepper grains, white
2 lemons
1 oz rosemary
5 1/2 oz oil
salt as desired

Choose preferably one single fish large enough to make one roast. Clean and wash it thoroughly, remove scales by scraping fish with a knife and rub with salt inside and outside. Heat oil in a saucepan or preferably in an oval roaster. Brown fish for 5 minutes on each side then place in moderate oven for 30 to 45 minutes.
If small fishes are used, 15 minutes will be sufficient.
Baste frequently with liquid in pan.
Heat white wine in a small pot, add crushed pepper grains and rosemary and allow to boil until wine is reduced to one pint. Remove fish from oven and arrange on serving platter. Sprinkle drippings remained in roaster with flour and reheat constantly stirring until flour becomes brown.
Pour heated wine and allow to boil constantly stirring for 3 minutes. Remove from heat and add lemon juice. Check salt and strain sauce through a sieve.
Scald and sprinkle over fish. Serve with boiled dandelion seasoned with lemon and oil.

JUMBO
SHRIMPS
ST DANIEL'S

To serve 6 persons

2 lbs jumbo shrimps
4 tablespoons brandy
1/2 lb San Daniele ham
30 mint leaves, fresh
5 1/2 oz butter
2 lemons
10 1/2 oz rice
1 pinch pepper
salt as desired

Shell shrimps, wash and clean thoroughly being careful to remove intestinal vein running length of body. Drain and pat dry. Marinate in a bowl with pepper and brandy for half hour. Cut ham into as many strips as the number of shrimps.
Wrap shrimps in ham and fill skewers intercalating one mint leaf. Pierce 4 to 5 shrimps on each skewer depending on actual size of shrimps. Heat 3 1/2 oz butter in a pan and arrange skewers. Cook for 3 minutes on each side then sprinkle with lemon juice. Reduce heat and simmer for a few minutes longer frequently basting with liquid in pan.
Cook rice, season with remaining butter and serve with shrimps.
Use Westphalian instead of San Daniele ham and basil leaves instead of mint.

LOBSTER
FRA DIAVOLO

To serve 6 persons

6 lbs lobster
3 oz butter
4 1/2 oz oil
3 oz garlic
1 lb tomatoes, fresh or canned
1/2 lb tomato purée
1 teaspoon origan
1 teaspoon crushed red pepper
pod
salt as desired

Cut lobster tail into 1-inch pieces without removing shell.
Cut head into halves lengthwise. Heat oil and butter in pan,
arrange lobster pieces and allow to brown until reddish.
Add chopped garlic and salt. Cook for 2 minutes then add
peeled and chopped tomatoes.
Cook for 10 minutes longer and pour tomato purée. Simmer
for 15 minutes until reduced and sprinkle with origan and
crushed red pepper. Cook 5 minutes longer and serve with
rice or noodles or with little toasts rubbed with garlic.

SWORD
FISH
ROLLS
PUNTA
FARO

To serve 6 persons
2 lbs sword fish
4 1/2 oz oil
2 oz pine nuts
1 oz onion
3 oz celery
2 tablespoons brandy
1 pinch minced marjoram
1/2 lb fresh bread crumbs
2 eggs

4 1/2 oz Swiss cheese
1 pinch origan
1 lemon
3 tablespoons chopped parsley
1 clove garlic
1 pinch pepper
salt as desired

Cut sword fish into 18 slices, three per person. Pound lightly with block. Trim off irregular bits and reserve for filling. Heat 2 oz oil in a saucepan and add chopped onion and celery, sauté for 10 to 15 minutes until tender then add reserved bits of fish finely chopped. Brown for 2 to 3 minutes and remove from heat. Add bread crumbs, diced Swiss cheese, marjoram, eggs, salt and mix well.
Sauté pine nuts in 1 1/2 oz oil until slightly brown, drain, squeeze or chop and add to filling. Split filling into 18 balls and arrange on fish slices. Sprinkle with salt and pepper and fold left and right side of fillets over filling then roll opposite sides to shape a kind of sausage thus enclosing stuffing firmly inside fillets. Arrange three rolls con two skewers. Reheat oil used to brown pine nuts in a larger pan add squeezed garlic and brown fish rolls for 10 minutes over low heat. Sprinkle with brandy.
Combine remaining oil, chopped parsley, origan and lemon juice and mix until blended. Remove squeezed garlic and pour sauce over rolls and serve at once.
Garnish with mint flavored peas.

FILLETS OF SOLE CALIFORNIA STYLE

To serve 6 persons

2 lbs fresh fillets of sole or 2
1/2 lbs frozen
2 oranges
2 grapefruits
2 avocados
2 lemons
salt to taste
1 teaspoon pepper
6 1/2 oz butter or margarine
Dredging flour

Peel oranges and grapefruit, cut into segments with a
sharpened knife removing skins in between pulps.
Remove stones from avocados and cut into slices. Arrange
fruits in a bowl together.
Beat eggs slightly and add a pinch of salt. Heat butter in
pan. Rub fillets of sole with salt and pepper, dredge with
flour and dip into beaten eggs. Remove any excess of egg
and fry over low heat for 5 minutes on each side.
Arrange fried fillets on serving platter. Drain avocado slices,
dredge with flour and dip in beaten eggs then fry in butter
remained in pan. Arrange two avocado slices on each fillet
and garnish with orange and grapefruit segments. Sprinkle
with lemon juice and serve well hot.

POACHED BROOK TROUT WITH VEGETABLES, FOAMY SAUCE

To serve 6 persons

6 brook trouts, 1/2 lb each
1/2 lb onions
1/2 lb celery
1/2 lb tomatoes
1/2 lb carrots
2 oz olive oil
1 lb potatoes
2 lemons
6 pepper grains
1 oz salt
3 quarts water
1 recipe Foamy Sauce (Recipe
N. 75)

Clean, pare and wash onions, carrots, potatoes and celery then cut into thin slices. Peel tomatoes, remove seeds and cut into quarters. Pour water in a casserole, add salt, pepper grains, lemon juice and oil. Heat to boiling and drop vegetables. Allow to cook until potatoes are done.

Remove all vegetables with skimmer and reserve in a covered bowl. Clean trouts and boil in vegetable broth for 2 minutes. Remove casserole from heat, cover and let stand trouts in water for 10 minutes longer. Drain and serve with cooked vegetables and foamy sauce.

Alternatively use mayonnaise instead of foamy sauce or blend in olive oil, lemon juice, dash of pepper and chopped parsley and pour over fish.

FILLETS
OF FLOUNDER
JOSEPHINE BAKER

To serve 6 persons

2 lbs fillets of flounder
3 eggs
6 1/2 oz oil
1/2 lb onions
1/2 lb tomatoes
1/2 lb green peppers
1 pinch black pepper
3 bananas
1 lemon
salt as desired
Dredging flour
Bread crumbs

135

Slightly beat eggs with a pinch of salt. Cut bananas into halves lengthwise and sprinkle with half lemon juice.

Cut onions into thin slices; peel tomatoes, remove seeds and chop coarsely. Clean peppers, remove seeds and cut into thin strips. Rub fish fillets with salt and pepper, dredge with flour, dip in beaten eggs and in bread crumbs.

Heat oil in a frying pan, dip banana halves in beaten eggs and dredge with flour then fry for 2 minutes or until golden brown. Drain on a plate. Continue frying prepared fish fillets. Drain and keep warm.

Sauté sliced onions in oil remained in pan for 5 minutes then add peppers and cook 5 minutes longer. Add tomatoes and cook for another 5 minutes adding salt if necessary.

Arrange fillets on serving platter, garnish with fried bananas and prepared sauce and sprinkle remaining lemon juice over fish.

WHITEFISH IN PAPER CASES BELVEDERE

To serve 6 persons

3 lbs whitefish
5 1/2 oz boiled ham, lean and fat
1/2 lb mushrooms
1 lb potatoes
2 oz onions
2 oz parsley
1/2 lb tomatoes

6 sprigs dill
2 oz butter
1 teaspoon pepper
Salt to taste
5 1/2 oz oil
Dredging flour

Clean fish and rub with salt inside and outside. Place sprigs of dill in the cavity of fish and dredge with flour.

Heat oil in pan and brown fish on both sides for 15 to 20 minutes. Remove from pan and arrange on platter.

Blend 1 oz butter with remaining oil in pan, add finely chopped onions and brown for 5 minutes. Add diced ham and mushrooms. Cook slowly for 5 minutes occasionally stirring then add chopped tomatoes and salt. Cook 10 minutes longer and sprinkle with chopped parsley and pepper.

Cook diced potatoes in salted water.

Cut a sheet of aluminum foil or parchment paper to shape a heart large enough to contain fish, line baking pan with foil or paper and melt in remaining butter. Spread a layer of prepared sauce and arrange fish; coat with remaining sauce and surround with potatoes. Enclose all ingredients by rolling edges of foil or paper tightly to prevent steam from escaping during cooking. Bake in moderate oven for 10 minutes until paper inflates. Serve directly from pan cutting enclosure in front of guests.

HALIBUT STEAK IN CASSEROLE A LA CORSARA

To serve 6 persons

3 lbs halibut steaks
1/2 lb onions
1/2 lb celery
1/2 lb tomatoes
2 lbs potatoes
2 oz capers
1 oz salt
1 teaspoon pepper
5 1/2 oz olive oil
1 quart water

Thoroughly clean and wash fish steaks and allow to drain. Combine sliced onions, sliced celery, minced capers, coarsely chopped tomatoes, oil, salt and pepper in a casserole large enough to contain fish as well. Cover with water and heat to boiling for 10 minutes. Add pared and sliced potatoes and boil for 5 minutes longer. Add fish steaks and more water if sauce thickens. Cover and cook for 15 minutes over moderate heat. Arrange steaks on serving platter and surround with sauce.

To vary, use other fish instead of halibut.

137

BAKED SNAILS WITH SAVORY BUTTER

To serve 6 to 12 persons

3 1/2 oz parsley
1 teaspoon salt
2 cloves garlic
1 lemon
2 bay leaves
5 1/2 oz butter
6 dozens snails, canned with
separated shells

Combine butter, salt and lemon juice in a bowl. Scrape bay leaves surfaces with a knife thus removing a sort of greenish paste and add to butter. If dried bay leaves are used, add just one pinch of finely ground leaf. Finely chop parsley leaves and garlic and blend in with butter. Work with a spatula until foamy.
Drain snails in a strainer and return to their shells.
Top opening with savory butter, evening with spatula.
Use snail cooker for best results or arrange snails in pan with openings upwards one close to the other to prevent their upsetting. Bake in oven until butter begins to froth. Snails can be prepared ahead of time and stored in refrigerator prior to baking.

Variation: Drain snails and sauté in a little butter adding chopped scallion. Three minutes after sprinkle with half glass dry white wine and simmer until evaporated. Add three tablespoons Sauce Marinara (Recipe N. 65), stir well and return snails to their shells proceeding as above.

FROG LEGS SAUTEED A LA PROVENÇALE

To serve 6 persons

3 lbs frog legs
2 oz garlic
3 oz parsley
4 lemons
1 glass dry white wine
6 1/2 oz olive oil
salt as desired
1 teaspoon white pepper
Dredging flour

Wash frog legs and arrange in a bowl. Sprinkle with salt, pepper and juice of 3 lemons. Marinate for one hour turning legs every 15 minutes.

Remove frog legs from marinade and dredge with flour until completely dry. Heat 5 1/2 oz oil in a pan and brown frog legs for 5 minutes. Pour white wine and let evaporate completely. Combine remaining oil in a skillet with chopped garlic and parsley and sauté until garlic flavor is smelt. Pour over frog legs and simmer 5 minutes longer to enhance flavor. Sprinkle with remaining lemon juice and serve with boiled rice seasoned with butter.

TENDERLOIN
OF BEEF
WELLINGTON

To serve 6 persons

2 lbs beef tenderloin
2 oz oil
4 1/2 oz goose liver
5 1/2 oz cooked ham slices
3 1/2 oz butter or margarine
7 oz flour
salt as desired
1 pinch pepper
2 bay leaves
1 egg

Choose center of beef tenderloin preferably. Remove fat and skin being careful not to tear flesh. Rub with salt and pepper and brown in a pan with oil and bay leaves for 20 minutes. Turn it over occasionally so that it browns on all sides. Remove from heat and allow to cool then evenly spread goose liver all around. If goose liver is not available use paté of pork or veal or chicken livers previously sautéed with onion and finely chopped. Wrap tenderloin with cooked ham slices then wrap it with dough following directions given below for its preparation.

Place in a shallow baking pan and brush surface with slightly beaten egg. Bake in hot oven for 15 minutes or until dough is golden brown. Remove from oven and let stand 5 minutes before slicing.

Dough: Combine flour, a pinch of salt, butter or margarine and a little water. Knead until mixture holds together and roll it thin then wrap tenderloin.
Serve with meat gravy (Recipe N. 59) and sliced mushrooms.
Garnish with watercress, a little celery and tomato slices, oil and lemon dressing.

MIXED GRILL GARDEN OF MARY

To serve 6 persons

6 rib lamb chops
6 sliced veal liver
6 small sausages
6 beef fillet slices
6 bacon strips
6 ripe tomato halves
6 mushroom caps, medium sized
1/2 lb watercress
1 oz oil
salt, paprika and black pepper

Marinate rib lamb chops, beef fillet slices, tomato halves and mushroom caps with a pinch of salt, pepper, paprika and oil for 1 hour. Shortly before serving, broil or pan-broil over high heat beginning with sausage, then go on with mushrooms, tomatoes and lamb chops. As the latter are done, sauté bacon strips in a pan for a few minutes and remove.
Sauté liver slices in bacon drippings and at the same time broil beef fillets for 2 minutes on each side. Remember that beef fillet is tastier if rare cooked. Arrange mixed grill on serving platter in diagonal rows starting with liver topped with bacon strips, lamb chops, tomatoes, sausage, beef fillets and mushrooms. Split watercress into two halves, remove outer leaves and garnish both ends of platter.
Serve at once with fried potatoes and lemon.

SHANKS
OF VEAL
COUNTRYSIDE

To serve 4 persons

2 veal shanks
12 spring onions or small onions
2 carrots, medium sized
8 small potatoes
2 tomatoes
1 stalk celery
2 bay leaves
salt as desired
1 pinch pepper
2 oz oil
2 oz butter or margarine

Clean veal shanks and arrange in center of casserole.
Sprinkle with salt and pepper, add oil butter and bay leaves, cover and place in moderate oven. Allow to stew slowly for 1 1/2 hour until delicately browned. Every 10 minutes, baste with liquid in casserole or turn shanks over.
Wash celery and cut into 1 inch pieces, scrape carrots and cut into halves lengthwise, peel onions, pare potatoes, cut tomatoes in quarters. Wash all vegetables and drain.
As veal will have stewed for nearly 1 hour, remove from oven and surround with vegetables sprinkling a little salt to taste. Return to oven and finish stewing for 30 minutes occasionally basting.
To vary, use any kind of fresh vegetables in season such as mushrooms, artichokes, zucchini, etc.

CHICKEN
A LA
KING

To serve 4 persons

2 1/2 lbs hen or chicken
1 small carrot
1 small celery stalk
1 small onion
6 pepper grains
1 sprig thyme
2 oz butter
1 tablespoon flour
4 tablespoons heavy cream
1 glass Sherry or Marsala wine
salt as desired
1 pinch white pepper

Clean chicken or hen, wash and arrange in a pot. Cover with water and heat to boiling for 2 minutes. Drain and sprinkle with cold water. Return to pot and cover again with water, heat to boiling and skim surface. Add salt, carrot, celery, thyme, pepper grains and 3/4 of onion. Cook for 45 minutes if it's chicken or longer if it's hen. Remove from stock and allow to cool. Accurately bone chicken and cut meat into strips or thin slices or cubes. Strain stock and reserve in a warm place. Chop remaining onion not more than 1 tablespoon and sauté in butter for a few minutes until transparent. Add chicken and stir for a couple of minutes then dust with flour, stir for another 2 to 3 minutes and pour strained stock. Simmer for 10 minutes constantly stirring, add Sherry, cream, salt and white pepper. Allow to cook for another 2 minutes and serve at once. Garnish with buttered noodles or rice or with small hot toasts.
To vary, use mushroom slices, cooked ham, roasted peppers, asparagus tips all cut into strips and combined with chicken.
Another suggestion: butter a baking pan, spread an even layer of lasagnas (dried or fresh) on bottom, pour creamed chicken, flatten surface with a spoon, dust with Parmesan or Swiss cheese and nutmeg, dot with butter and bake until au gratin. Serve with hot Cranberry sauce.

BEEF TONGUE IN SAUERSWEET SAUCE

To serve 6 persons

4 to 6 lbs whole ox tongue	1 stick cinnamon, small
3 oz butter or margarine	2 oz sugar
1 onion, medium sized	4 1/2 oz vinegar
6 cloves	2 oz pine nuts
1 carrot and celery leaves	2 oz raisins
2 bay leaves	salt as desired
5 pepper grains	1 pinch aromatic herbs

Sauce: Melt butter in a saucepan and sauté sliced onion for 10 minutes over very low heat until transparent. Add cloves, bay leaves, pepper grains, cinnamon, sugar, vinegar, a glass of water and a pinch of salt. Cover and cook over hing heat for 15 minutes. Strain through a sieve and transfer in a small pot. Wash raisins and soak for 10 minutes. Drain and add to sauce. Sauté pine nuts in a skillet over low heat until browned and fold in sauce.

Arrange tongue in a pot and cover with plenty of water.

Heat to boiling for a few minutes, drain and sprinkle with cold water. Return tongue to pot, cover with fresh water, heat to boiling and skim surface. Add onion, salt, celery leaves, carrot and a pinch of aromatic herbs. Cover and simmer for 3 hours about. As tongue in done drain and sprinkle with cold water then skin with a knife. Cut into slices, arrange in a pan and coat with sauce. Allow to cook for a few minutes longer to gain flavor.

Use canned or smoked tongue for a speedier preparation.

Garnish with spinach, mashed potatoes or braised lentils.

Store leftover tongue in refrigerator to be served cold together with ham, chicken, turkey or on sandwich with a slice of Swiss cheese and a little mustard.

VEAL
SCALOPPINI
MILLY

To serve 4 persons

1 lb veal round or other tender
cuts
2 small zucchini
2 ripe tomatoes, medium sized
1 clove garlic
2 eggs
Dredging flour
1 pinch pepper
salt as desired
1 pinch sugar
3 oz ham or lean saltpork
2 oz oil
3 oz butter or margarine
1/2 oz fresh basil or 1
teaspoon dried soaked in
water

Cut veal round into four slices per person and pound them thin. Peel tomatoes, remove seeds
and cut into small strips.
Peel zucchini, and cut into slices crosswise, sprinkle with a pinch of salt, dredge with flour, dip
in beaten egg and brown in a skillet with oil for 3 to 4 minutes. Remove from pan and drain on
a plate. Add 1 oz butter in skillet, put in squeezed garlic and add ham cut into thin strips.
Sauté until garlic flavor in smelt then add tomatoes, pepper, sugar and basil. Cook for 5
minutes and remove garlic.
Melt remaining butter in a pan, dredge scaloppini with flour, sprinkle with salt and cook for 3
minutes on each side. Arrange zucchini and scaloppini into four individual casseroles, pour
dripping from cooking scaloppini and prepared sauce. Scald and serve. Garnish with mashed
potatoes, flavored with chopped mint leaves.

GRILLED
HAM
RIVIERA

To serve 4 persons

4 ham slices, 4 1/2 oz each
1 tablespoon powdered mustard
Bread crumbs
1/2 lb cherries
4 oranges
4 lemons
2 oz butter

Blend powdered mustard in half glass of water. Spread it evenly on ham slices to coat them completely. Dip in bread crumbs slightly pressing with a knife blade so as crumbs adhere. Sprinkle with melted butter. Broil slices on a grill or pan-broil until golden brown over low heat.
Cut peeled oranges and lemons into segments, stone cherries.
Combine together in a pan and scald for a few minutes.
Arrange ham slices on platter and garnish with fruit.
Serve at once with fried potatoes.
To vary, use fresh fruit in season or any canned fruit following same directions.
Another variation, serve ham slices with fried potatoes and separately serve lettuce hearts topped with orange and lemon segments seasoning with a few drops of oil, salt and pepper.

CREAMED
PHEASANT
MARBELIA

To serve 4 persons

2 pheasants, 2 1/2 lbs each
salt as desired
10 pepper grains
5 cloves
3 bay leaves
2 glasses dry white wine
6 1/2 oz butter
2 oz onions
1 oz carrots
1 oz leeks

1 sprig thyme
5 juniper berries
1 lb heavy cream
6 tablespoons meat gravy
(Recipe N. 59)
1 lemon
1 pinch paprika
1/2 lb fresh mushrooms
1/2 lb rice

Cut pheasants in quarters and remove bones. Wash and arrange in a bowl, add salt, pepper grains, cloves, bay leaves and sprinkle with white wine. Let stand to marinate for 1 hour. Melt 4 1/2 oz butter in a casserole, add chopped onions, carrots and leeks, add thyme and juniper berries.

As soon as butter begins to froth, drain pheasants, reserving marinade, and put in casserole. Stir for a few minutes, cover and cook over low heat. When pheasants begin to brown strain marinade and sprinkle over pheasants. Allow to evaporate and add heavy cream. Finish cooking over low heat for 3/4 hour or until pheasants are tender. Remove and transfer meat in a covered casserole. Add meat gravy to stock, sprinkle with paprika and lemon juice. Sieve sauce and pour over pheasants. Heat to boiling for 2 minutes and remove from heat. Dot with 3/4 oz butter and keep in a warm place.

Clean and wash mushrooms then cut into thin slices and brown in remaining butter. Spread mushrooms over pheasants and serve with cooked rice.

BEEF
IN
CASSEROLE
STROGONOFF

To serve 4 persons

2 lbs lean beef
2 cloves garlic
1 onion, medium sized
1/2 lb mushrooms
2 oz tomato paste
4 1/2 oz meat gravy or beef stock or water and beef extract
3 oz stoned olives
1 teaspoon Worcestershire sauce
4 tablespoons yoghourt or sour cream
1 glass Sherry wine
3 oz oil
salt as desired
2 oz butter
1 pinch black pepper
Dredging flour
2 bay leaves
1/2 oz Tarragon leaves

Cut beef into 1 inch cubes and dredge with flour. Heat 2 oz oil and 1 oz butter in a casserole and add beef. Stir until slightly brown then add coarsely chopped onion and bay leaves.
Sauté for another couple of minutes then add salt, pepper, tomato paste and continue browning for a few minutes. Sprinkle with 2 glasses of water, cover and cook over low heat occasionally stirring. If sauce thickens add more water. After nearly 1 hour meat should be done. Add meat gravy or beef stock or water with beef extract.
Clean mushrooms and cut into thin slices. Heat remaining oil and butter in a saucepan, add chopped garlic, mushrooms and salt. Sauté for a few minutes. As meat is done, remove from sauce, transfer in another casserole, coat with mushrooms, sliced olives and chopped tarragon leaves. Press sauce through a sieve, pour over meat and boil for 2 minutes. Remove from heat, pour sour cream or yoghourt, Worcestershire Sauce, add salt if necessary and sprinkle with Sherry wine. Serve at once with cooked rice or egg noodles.
For a quicker preparation use tender meat cuts such as fillet instead of beef.

VEAL
KIDNEYS
PIAZZA
NAVONA

To serve 4 persons

1 1/4 lbs veal kidneys
5 1/2 oz butter
1 oz oil
1 tablespoon mustard
2 cloves garlic
2 oz parsley leaves
2 tablespoons vinegar or dry white wine
1 lb peas, fresh or canned
6 artichokes, fresh or canned
1 oz mint leaves
1 small onion
salt as desired
1 pinch pepper
1 teaspoon sugar

Cut kidneys into halves, remove fat and skin, wash them thoroughly and cut into slices. Put kidneys in a pan and heat slowly for a few minutes to release water. Drain and wash again. Heat 3 oz butter and oil in pan and add chopped garlic, kidneys and salt and allow to cook over high heat for 5 minutes. Blend mustard in vinegar and sprikle over kidneys together with chopped parsley. Cook for 2 minutes longer, remove from heat and garnish with prepared peas and artichokes.
Remove woody parts from artichokes and split into sixths lengthwise. Combine artichokes and peas in a casserole, add chopped onion, salt, pepper, sugar and 2 oz butter.
Sprinkle with a glass of water, cover and cook for half hour then add chopped mint leaves. If mixture turns out to be too liquid, remove lid and cook until evaporated.

APPETIZING ROCK CORNISH GAME HEN

To serve 4 persons
2 to 4 game hens, depending
on size
4 1/2 oz oil
salt as desired
1 pinch pepper
1 oz onion
1 oz celery
2 cloves garlic
3 oz stoned black olives
1/2 lb mushrooms
1 pinch origan
1 lemon
1 glass brandy or Cognac

Split hens into quarters, remove bones and rub with salt and pepper. Heat oil in a broad pan and arrange hens.
Allow to brown on all sides. Remove oil from pan and pour it in another pan. Sprinkle brandy over hens, heat for 1 minute and ignite. When blazing is extinguished remove from heat. Reheat oil and add chopped onion and minced celery, sauté for a few minutes then add chopped garlic, hens and origan. Cover and cook for 1/2 hour over low heat then add olives and sliced mushrooms previously dipped in lemon juice. Cook 5 minutes longer or until legs are tender and serve with cooked rice or mixed cooked vegetables or corn fritters.

BRAISED OXTAIL APPIA ANTICA

To serve 4 persons

3 lbs oxtail
2 oz oil
Dredging flour
salt as desired
5 black pepper grains
1 stalk celery
1 small carrot
1 small onion
1 sprig thyme
2 lemon peels (yellow rind only)
1 clove garlic
2 oz parsley
1 glass red wine
2 oz tomato paste

Cut oxtail through the joints with a sharpened knife and remove fat if present. Heat oil in a pan add oxtail dredged with flour and allow to brown well. Combine butter, diced carrot, celery and onion in a casserole and sauté for a few minutes. Add oxtail, salt, crushed pepper grains and thyme. Sprinkle with red wine and allow to evaporate completely. Add tomato paste and stir until dissolved then pour water to cover oxtail. Cover and simmer for 3 hours occasionally stirring. Add a little water during cooking if sauce thickens. Remove oxtail and transfer in another casserole. Press sauce through a sieve and pour it over oxtail. Reheat, check salt and skim surface of sauce. Add finely chopped lemon peels, parsley and garlic. Cook for 10 minutes longer and serve.
Garnish with mashed potatoes or mint flavored peas or beans.
Oxtail may be prepared ahead of time and scalded just before serving, in this way it acquires an even better taste.

VEAL SCALOPPINI DUCA DI NORCIA

To serve 4 persons

8 scaloppini, 2 oz each
3 oz butter
Dredging flour
24 black truffles slices or 8 mushroom caps
1 tablespoon Madeira or Marsala wine
1/2 lb Swiss cheese or Fontina
2 egg yolks
1 pinch white pepper
4 tablespoons milk or water

Fondue: Cut Swiss cheese or Fontina into dice and combine in a pot with 1 oz butter, pepper, egg yolks and milk.
Place pot in a pan of hot water and stir constantly. At first mixture will become thick, then it will melt and finally it will become creamy almost like mayonnaise. Remove from hot water immediately.
Melt 2 oz butter in a pan, dredge scaloppini with flour and cook for 4 to 5 minutes on each side. Arrange scaloppini in a casserole and coat with prepared fondue. Top scaloppini with 3 truffles slices each, previously marinated in Madeira or Marsala wine. Serve at once well hot with toasts.
Use mushroom caps instead of truffles. Leave caps whole and sauté in butter.

PORK SKEWERS GRAND MOTHER'S WAY

153

To serve 4 persons

1 lb loin of pork, boned
1/2 lb bacon strips
8 bay leaves or sage leaves
1 oz oil
1 oz butter
salt as desired
1 clove garlic
1 pinch black pepper
1 pinch fennel seeds

Polenta
1 1/2 quart water
1/2 lb corn meal
1 lb broccoli
2 tablespoons oil
1/2 oz salt
1 pinch allspice

Remove excess of fat from loin leaving just a little. Cut into slices and arrange in a bowl with sliced bacon, pepper, fennel seeds, oil, sage or bay leaves, salt and squeezed garlic. Marinate for at least 2 hours.
Prepare skewers piercing a slice of bacon a sage leaf, a slice of loin and repeat with this order to fill 4 skewers.
Melt butter in pan, arrange skewers and allow to brown for 5 minutes. Sprinkle with marinade and cook for 10 minutes longer. Serve with green corn meal.
Green corn meal. Heat salted water to boiling, add coarsely chopped broccoli and oil. Cook until broccoli are done.
Add corn meal, stir and cook for half hour or just a few minutes if precooked corn meal is used. Stir frequently during cooking to prevent settling.

BABY
LAMB
CHOPS
MIMOSA

To serve 4 persons

12 lamb chops
1 lb bread crumbs
1 oz scallion
2 oz parsley
1/2 lb mushrooms
2 oz butter or margarine
3 oz oil
1 lb potatoes
1 clove garlic
1/2 lb zucchini

Fat for frying
2 1/2 oz Strained Tomato sauce (Recipe N. 60)
2 1/2 oz Meat gravy (Recipe N. 59)
salt as desired
1 pinch pepper
2 eggs
Dredging flour
3 tablespoons milk

Pound lamb chops as thin as possible. Remove any fatty or nervous tissues. Finely chop scallion, parsley and mushrooms and combine with sifted bread crumbs. Pare potatoes, wash and cut into thin slices. Cook in a pan with 1 oz oil, 1 oz butter, squeezed garlic and a pinch of salt. Peel zucchini and cut into thin strips, dip in milk and dredge with flour. Remove excess flour and fry in hot deep fat until golden brown. Beat eggs with pepper and salt. Rub lamb chops with salt, dredge with flour, dip in beaten egg and in bread crumb mixture. Press chops with a spatula so as crumbs adhere. Heat remaining oil and butter in a pan and cook lamb chops for 5 minutes on each side. Arrange on serving platter garnishing with prepared potatoes and zucchini. Separately serve tomato sauce blended with an equal amount of meat gravy.
For a quicker preparation, serve lamb chops only with a mint flavored salad.

VEAL MEDALLIONS AU GRATIN HOMERIC

To serve 4 persons

1 lb veal fillet or other tender cuts
1/2 lb Sauce Cacciatora (Recipe N. 55)
12 thin slices Swiss cheese
1 pinch chopped tarragon leaves
2 lbs asparagus tips, fresh or 1 lb canned
3 oz butter
Dredging flour
salt as desired
1 pinch pepper
Grated Parmesan or Swiss cheese

Cut veal into 8 thin slices. Rub with salt and pepper, dredge with flour and cook for 4 minutes on each side in 2 oz melted butter.

Arrange 2 slices each into four individual casseroles, coat with Sauce Cacciatora, sprinkle with chopped tarragon leaves and top with 3 Swiss cheese slices. Pour remaining butter from cooking veal and place in oven for a few minutes or until cheese melts.

Serve at once with buttered asparagus tips sprinkled with grated Parmesan or Swiss cheese.

BREAST
OF
CAPON
CORDON
BLEU

To serve 2 persons

4 breasts of capon
2 slices cooked ham
2 slices Swiss cheese
1 egg
Dredging flour
Bread crumbs

2 oz butter
6 small tomatoes
1 lb cooked spinach
1/2 lb spring potatoes, roasted
1/2 lemon
1 scallion, small
1/2 oz parsley

Cut capon legs, remove skin from breast and cut wings up to the first joint. Divide breast into two parts, cut it lengthwise through the center near bone to remove flesh easily. Remove fillets from inside breast halves and reserve.

Delicately pound breasts with a block sprinkling with a little water until as thin as possible. Arrange one ham and one Swiss cheese slice inside breasts. Pound reserved fillets and remove center nerve with a knife or simply strip it away.

Arrange fillets as well inside breasts. Gently press with knife's blade and slightly pound with dull edge of knife.

Rub with salt, dredge with flour, dip in beaten eggs and in bread crumbs. Gently press again so as crumbs adhere.

Heat butter and chopped scallion in pan, arrange breasts and cook over low heat for 7 to 8 minutes on each side or until golden brown.

Arrange cooked spinach in center of platter, place breasts on top and surround with roasted potatoes and tomatoes sautéed for 2 minutes in breasts drippings. Sprinkle lemon juice and chopped parsley over breasts and serve.

VEAL

SCALOPPINI

VITTORIA

To serve 4 persons

1 lb veal leg or other tender
cuts
1 lb eggplants
2 eggs
1 teaspoon marjoram
salt as desired
1 pinch pepper
1/2 clove garlic
1 lb potatoes
4 1/2 oz oil
2 oz butter
1 lemon
Dredging flour
1 oz grated Parmesan or Swiss
cheese
Fat for frying potatoes

Cut veal into 8 slices. Pound with a block 1/4 inch thin. Combine eggs, a pinch of salt, pepper, chopped garlic, marjoram and grated cheese in a bowl. Mix until blended. Peel eggplants and cut into slices crosswise. Pare potatoes and cut into 1/4 inch wide strips then fry in hot deep fat. Heat oil in a pan, slightly dredge eggplants with flour, dip in beaten egg mixture, drain and cook for 5 minutes on each side. Cook scaloppini same as eggplants then arrange on serving platter with fried potatoes and eggplants. Sprinkle with lemon and browned butter.

RIBS
OF
BEEF
GROTTA
AZZURRA

To serve 2 to 4 persons

2 lbs rib's steaks
2 oz oil
2 cloves garlic
1 lb ripe tomatoes
salt as desired
1 pinch origan
1 pinch pepper
Mashed potatoes au gratin

Dip ripe tomatoes in boiling water for 2 minutes then sprinkle with cold water to peel them easily. Cut into halves, remove seeds and reserve.

Heat oil in a pan, brown steaks for 6 minutes on each side over high heat. Remove from heat and reserve steaks on a plate in a warm place. Add squeezed garlic in pan and sauté for 1 minute, add chopped tomatoes, salt, pepper and origan. Cook for 10 minutes over high heat then add steaks and released drippings. Cook for 2 minutes longer and serve with mashed potatoes au gratin.

Mashed potatoes au gratin: Prepare mashed potatoes without milk. Place in a buttered pan, flatten surface with a spoon, sprinkle with grated cheese and dot with butter. Bake in oven until au gratin.

SWEETBREADS IN CASSEROLE, PORT WINE

To serve 4 persons

1 1/2 lbs sweetbreads, veal,
beef or lamb
1 lemon
1 teaspoon salt
2 bay leaves
5 pepper grains
2 oz butter
2 oz carrots
2 lbs spinach
2 oz celery
4 tablespoons Port Wine
3 oz heavy cream

Soak sweetbreads in cold water for a few hours. Remove skins and membranes. Arrange in a pot, cover with water, add salt, lemon juice, bay leaves and pepper grains. Heat to boiling for 15 minutes, remove from heat and allow to cool. Drain and remove any membranes that may have come out during cooking. Melt butter in a pan, add chopped celery and carrots and sauté for a few minutes. Add sweetbreads, allow to brown for 5 minutes then sprinkle with Port wine. As soon as wine is evaporated pour heavy cream.
Cover and place in moderate oven for 15 minutes or until golden brown. Serve at once with buttered spinach or asparagus tips, or mushrooms or peas or rice.

CHICKEN CACCIATORA PRINCE OF VALDIERI

To serve 4 persons

4 lbs chicken
1 lb ripe tomatoes
1/2 lb mushrooms
4 1/2 oz onions
2 bay leaves
1 oz butter
1 sprig thyme
4 1/2 oz oil
1 glass dry white wine
salt as desired
1 pinch pepper
1 lb noodles
Dredging flour
1 1/2 oz parsley

Remove chicken legs and cut into halves by the joints. Cut breasts and split into quarters. Remove as many bones as possible leaving only large bones of legs and wings. Wash all pieces and drain. Peel ripe tomatoes, cut into halves remove seeds then chop very finely. Clean mushrooms, wash under running water and cut into slices. Put mushrooms on a plate and coat them with 2 tablespoons chopped tomatoes.
Heat oil and butter in a casserole, rub chicken with salt and dredge with flour then arrange in pan and sauté until brown. Add chopped onions and cook 5 minutes longer over low heat constantly stirring. Pour white wine and continue cooking until evaporated. Add bay leaves, pepper, thyme and chopped tomatoes. Cover and cook for 15 minutes over low heat adding a little water if sauce thickens. Add mushrooms, stir and allow to cook for 15 minutes longer occasionally stirring. Remove bay leaves, add finely chopped parsley and serve with buttered noodles.

VEAL

STEAK

PARMIGIANA

To serve 4 persons

1 lb veal shank or other tender
cuts
2 eggs
Dredging flour
Bread crumbs
1/2 lb Basil flavored tomato
pulp (Recipe N. 63)
4 Mozzarella or Swiss cheese
slices
1 oz oil
2 oz butter
Grated Parmesan cheese
Salt and pepper to taste

Cut veal into four slices and pound with a block until 1/4
inch thin. Rub with salt and generously sprinkle with
pepper. Dredge with flour, dip in slightly beaten egg and
then in bread crumbs. Press with a knife's blade so as
crumbs adhere. Heat oil and 1 oz butter in pan and cook
steaks for 5 minutes each side or until golden brown.
Remove pan from heat and coat steaks with tomato pulp up
to 1 inch from rim. Cover with sliced Swiss cheese or
mozzarella, freely sprinkle with Parmesan cheese and dot
with remaining butter. Place in moderate oven for a few
minutes or until cheese melts through steaks. Serve at once
garnished with sautéd potatoes and broccoli.

TURKEY
IN
CASSEROLE
COLUMBIA

To serve 4 persons

2 lbs young turkey
1/2 lb onions
4 1/2 oz parsley
2 oz pine nuts
salt as desired
1 pinch pepper
1 glass dry white wine
4 1/2 oz oil
1 pinch powdered cinnamon
1/2 lb mushrooms
2 bay leaves

Cut turkey into 1 inch cubes, remove small bones and leave skin. Coarsely chop onions and parsley. Combine turkey, salt, pepper, onions, parsley, bay leaves and cinnamon.
Mix thoroughly. Heat oil in a casserole and brown pine nuts; remove with skimmer or basting spoon and reserve.
Arrange turkey mixture in casserole and stir. Cover and stir occasionally until browned. When sauce thickens pour white wine, cover and continue simmering for 3/4 hour adding some water as necessary to prevent sauce from overthickening.
Clean mushrooms and cut into quarters, sprinkle them with salt and fold into casserole together with pine nuts.
Allow to cook 15 minutes longer then check if turkey is well done. If not add more water if necessary cover and continue simmering. On the contrary, if turkey is done, and sauce is too liquid, remove lid and allow to evaporate.
At the end of cooking sauce must be smooth and rather thick. Serve with cooked vegetables or mashed potatoes mixed with chives stewed in butter.

GOLDEN CALF'S BRAINS, CAULIFLOWER & ARTICHOKES HENRY

163

To serve 4 persons

1 1/2 lb calf's brains
4 artichokes
1 cauliflower, medium sized
Dredging flour
4 eggs
1/2 lb oil
1 oz butter

salt as desired
1 pinch pepper
1 lemon
1 oz parsley
2 tablespoons white vinegar
2 bay leaves

Soak calf's brains in cold water for a few hours. Drain and remove skins, membranes and blood vessels. Arrange in a pot, add 1 teaspoon salt, vinegar and bay leaves. Cover with water and heat to boiling then simmer for 15 minutes. Allow to cool and drain. Cut brains into thin slices and reserve.

At the same time boil cauliflower in salted water for 15 minutes or anyhow underdone. Drain and cool. Cut cauliflower into pieces large as a walnut and get rid of the stem.

Clean artichokes, remove outer leaves and trim inner ones.

Cut into thin slices and dip in a little water with half lemon juice. Slightly beat eggs with a pinch of salt and pepper.

Heat oil in frying pan, drain artichokes, dredge with flour, dip in beaten eggs and remove any excess then fry over moderate heat for 10 minutes. Remove with skimmer and allow to drain on a grate. Proceed as above for frying brains and cauliflower.

Arrange on serving platter heaping cauliflowers in center and surround with an alternate row of brains and artichokes.

Sprinkle brains with finely chopped parsley and remaining lemon juice. Brown butter in a skillet and pour over brains.

Use any other vegetable in season instead of cauliflower and artichokes or likewise use pork or lamb brains.

MIXED BOILED POT ITALIAN STYLE

To serve 6 persons

2 lbs brisket of beef	6 leeks
1 veal shank	6 small carrots
1 lb calf's head	6 small turnips
6 sausages	6 small potatoes
2 1/4 lb chicken	1 stalk celery
1 veal tongue	salt as desired
1 lb cabbage	6 white pepper grains

Pour 5 quarts water in a stockpot and add 1 tablespoon salt.

Heat to boiling and drop meats except head and tongue. As soon as boiling is resumed skim surface and drop green part of leeks, celery leaves and crushed pepper grains. Simmer for 3/4 hour then remove chicken if done. Cook half hour longer and remove veal shank then allow another half hour before removing brisket of beef. Separately cook calf's head and tongue following same procedure. Head is well done when it is easily pierced by a fork and tongue when it is tender.

Remove head and clean it inside then reserve in stock. Remove tongue, cool and skin it without tearing flesh apart.

While meats are cooking remove outer leaves from cabbage, scrap carrots and peel turnips, split celery into sixths, pare potatoes. Thoroughly wash all vegetables together with leeks. Arrange all vegetables in a pan and keep separated, sprinkle with salt and pour 3 ladles of stock from cooking meats, as soon as veal shank has been removed. Cover and cook slowly for half hour. Be careful to keep heat low so as vegetables won't dissolve.

Cook sausages in salted water over low heat.

Just before serving arrange meats in a large pan, sprinkle with a little stock and heat to boiling. Serve with prepared vegetables and, if desired, with three color sauces.

Red Sauce: Use strained tomato sauce (Recipe N. 60) or Tomato Katchup.

White Sauce: Whip 1 glass heavy cream with 1 pinch of salt until fluffy. Add 1 pinch pepper, 1 tablespoon vinegar and 1 tablespoon rasped horseradish.

Green Sauce: Combine 3 oz parsley, 3 cloves of garlic, 4 anchovy fillets, 2 oz pickles, 1 crushed pepper pod and 3 oz fresh bread crumb soaked in vinegar and squeezed.
Chop all above ingredients as finely as possible, add a pinch of pepper and salt. Put in a bowl and blend with 3 tablespoons oil and 2 tablespoons vinegar. Mix until creamy.

VEAL CHOPS IN PIQUANTE SAUCE

165

To serve 6 persons

6 veal chops
3 tablespoon white vinegar
3 anchovy fillets
2 gherkins
1 tablespoon capers
1 clove garlic
1 oz parsley leaves
salt as desired
1 pinch pepper
Dredging flour
3 oz butter

Melt butter in a pan large enough to contain all chops.
Rub veal chops with salt and sprinkle with pepper. Dredge with flour and cook over moderate heat without browning. Chop anchovies, gherkins, capers, garlic and parsley.
Heat vinegar in a skillet for 2 to 3 minutes and add chopped ingredients. Allow to boil for another couple of minutes and pour over chops. Cook for a few minutes longer continuously basting chops with sauce in pan. Serve at once.

CHICKEN AND SAUSAGE EN BROCHETTE WITH RED CABBAGE

Orange stewed cabbage
2 lbs red cabbage
2 oz salt pork, bacon or margarine
salt as desired
1 pinch pepper
4 cloves
2 apples
1 tablespoon flour
1 pinch powdered cinnamon
1 tablespoon sugar
1 tablespoon red vinegar
2 oranges

To serve 4 persons

1 lb boneless chicken
1/2 lb sausages
3 peppers, medium sized
12 mushrooms, medium sized
1 teaspoon mustard
salt as desired
2 oz butter or margarine

Cut chicken and sausage into 1 inch pieces. Cut peppers into halves, remove seeds, wash and cut into 1 inch squares.

Clean mushrooms, separate caps and reserve stems for stewed cabbage. Sprinkle salt over chicken, peppers and mushrooms caps. Arrange on skewers beginning with a mushroom cap, a piece of chicken, a pepper square and a piece of sausage. Continue alternating pieces with the same order and close with a mushroom cap. Reserve skewers in a cool place to be cooked 20 minutes before serving. Melt butter in a pan, arrange skewers and cook over low heat for 15 minutes turning them regularly so as they can brown uniformly.

Remove skewers from pan and arrange on serving platter.

Add mustard to dripping in pan and a little water if necessary.

Heat to boiling then scrap bottom with a spoon or spatula and pour over skewers. Serve at once.

Orange stewed cabbage

Clean and wash cabbage, cut into thin strips. Melt fat in a pot and add cabbage, chopped mushroom stems, a pinch of salt, pepper, cloves, peeled and sliced apples and orange juice. Cover and stew for 5 minutes. Pour boiling water to cover cabbage and stew for half hour. Combine flour, sugar, cinnamon, vinegar and 1 teaspoon water in a bowl. Mix until well blended and pour over cabbage. Stir and allow to stew 10 minutes longer.

167

VEAL
STEW
AUNT LIDIA

To serve 6 persons

2 lbs veal stew
2 lbs spring onions
2 cloves garlic
3 bay leaves
1/2 lb ripe tomatoes
4 1/2 oz olive oil
1 pinch pepper
1 small cinnamon stick
salt as desired

Wash and peel spring onions. Cut veal stew into pieces matching onions. Combine veal and onions in a casserole add salt, bay leaves, cinnamon, pepper, olive oil, peeled and coarsely chopped tomatoes, squeezed whole garlic and enough water to cover. Allow to stew covered for nearly 1 hour over low heat. When veal is done remove lid and allow to evaporate any excess of water to the desired consistency.

GUINEA HEN IN CASSEROLE OCEANIC

To serve 6 persons
2 Guinea hens, 2 1/2 lb each
7 oz flour
2 oz oil
2 oz butter
2 glasses Madeira or Marsala wine
1 ladle meat gravy or beef stock
salt as desired

1 pinch pepper
2 oz goose liver
1 sprig thyme or 2 bay leaves
6 small carrots
3 small zucchini
6 small onions
12 small mushrooms
6 small potatoes
1 glass dry white wine
1 oz parsley leaves

Split Guinea hens into 8 pieces by cutting legs by the joints and breasts into quarters. Remove all small bones. Rub with salt and pepper. Heat butter and oil in a broad pan, large enough to contain all pieces on one layer. Dredge hen pieces with flour and allow to brown frequently stirring. Add thyme and stir for 2 to 3 minutes. Sprinkle with white wine and allow to evaporate then pour meat gravy or beef stock. Cook over low heat frequently stirring for 1/2 hour. Add onions and cook 30 minutes longer. Skim surface during cooking if necessary.

Meanwhile cut zucchini into quarters, scrap carrots, pare potatoes, clean mushrooms and leave whole. Wash all vegetables and combine in a pan with a pinch of salt and 1 tablespoon butter. Bake in moderate oven until done. Fold baked vegetables with hen and remove from heat. Blend goose liver with Marsala or Madeira wine and pour over hen. Sprinkle with chopped parsley and reserve covered in a warm place.

Make a dough with remaining flour and a little water.

Shape a stick with dough and seal lid and casserole as tightly as possible to prevent steam from escaping.

Ten minutes before serving, place casserole in oven and undo directly before guests.

For a better display cook hens in metal casseroles and transfer in a pyrex pan before last ten minutes baking.

SIRLOIN
OF
BEEF
FAVOURITE

To serve 4 persons

4 sirloin steaks, 1/2 lb each
1 teaspoon chopped scallion or chives
1/2 glass Sherry or dry white wine
1 teaspoon Worcestershire sauce
1/2 lemon
1/2 tablespoon mustard
3 oz butter
1 pinch freshly ground pepper
Green beans and potatoes as desired

169

Remove any fatty or nervous tissues from sirloin steaks.
Pound them as thin as possible. Brown 2 oz butter in a pan, and sauté steaks for 2 minutes on each side. Remove and drain. Reserve remaining butter in pan to season green beans. Pour wine in pan, add chopped scallion or chives and heat to boiling until wine is reduced to half. Blend 1 oz butter, juice of half lemon, Worcestershire sauce, mustard and pepper. Sprinkle steaks with salt and return to pan, scald for 2 minutes, remove from heat and pour prepared butter over steaks. Serve at once.
Garnish with fried potatoes and cooked green beans seasoned with reserved melted butter a pinch of grated cheese, a dash nutmeg and browned for 1 minutes.
To vary, proceed as above for browning sirloins, remove butter, sprinkle with a glass of Cognac or brandy, ignite and when flame is extinguished add prepared butter.

STUFFED BONELESS LEGS OF CHICKEN FAMOUS VITTORIO

To serve 6 persons

6 large chicken legs	1/2 pint milk	1 sprig thyme
1/2 lb pork meat	3 oz canned peas	Butter and oil
1/2 lb goose or chicken livers	1 oz black truffles (optional)	1 glass dry white wine
salt as desired	6 slices salt pork, thin	1/2 lb ripe tomatoes
1 pinch pepper	1 1/2 oz onions	1 ladle meat gravy (Recipe N. 59) or beef stock or water and beef extract
1 dash nutmeg	1 oz celery	
1/2 clove garlic	1 oz carrots	1 lb small potatoes
4 1/2 oz fresh bread crumb	2 bay leaves	1 1/2 oz parsley

Remove thigh bones from chicken legs and joint between thigh and drumstick. Spread flesh to enable stuffing.

Combine chopped pork meat, chopped goose liver or diced chicken livers previously browned, salt, pepper, nutmeg, finely chopped garlic, peas, diced truffles and bread crumb previously soaked in milk, squeezed and chopped. Mix thoroughly and fill chicken legs. Overlap flesh to prevent stuffing from escaping and wrap in salt pork slices. Select a pan large enough to contain all legs, combine 2 tablespoons butter and 2 tablespoons oil, chopped celery, onions and carrots, add bay leaves and thyme then arrange chicken legs. Place in moderate oven for 15 minutes. Remove from oven and drain drippings in a cup. Sprinkle legs with white wine and heat until wine is evaporated. Add chopped tomatoes and meat gravy, cover and return to oven for 1/2 hour frequently basting with liquid in pan. Remove from oven and transfer legs into another pan. Skim sauce if necessary and strain through a sieve.

Brown diced potatoes in a pan using reserved drippings for 20 minutes about.

Arrange chicken legs on serving platter, surround with browned potatoes and coat with strained sauce. Just before serving sprinkle with chopped parsley. Garnish with mint flavored peas or buttered asparagus or artichoke quarters.

VEAL SCALOPPINI ROMAN STYLE

To serve 4 persons

8 scaloppini, 2 oz each
Salt and pepper as desired
8 sage leaves
8 ham slices thin
5 oz butter
1/2 glass white wine
1/2 lemon
Dredging flour
1 lb shelled or canned peas
5 mint leaves
1 pinch sugar

Pound scaloppini and rub with salt and pepper to taste.
Place a sage leaf in center and top with a ham slice.
Secure both sage and ham with a skewer. Dredge with flour.
Heat 3 oz butter in a pan and brown scaloppini for 2 minutes on ham side and for 5 minutes on opposite side. Remove and keep in a warm place. Pour white wine in pan, add lemon juice and scrap bottom of pan with a spoon to loosen any settled dripping. Pour over scaloppini and serve at once.
Garnish with buttered peas sprinkled with sugar and finely chopped mint leaves.

DUCKLING IN ORANGE SAUCE

172

To serve 4 to 8 persons

2 ducklings, 4 lbs each
2 oz butter or margarine
3 oz sugar
4 tablespoons vinegar
1 tablespoon cornstarch
2 tablespoon guava jelly or orange
1 orange per person plus 1 for sauce

3 tablespoons Curaçao
1 oz carrots
1 oz onion
1 sprig thyme
1 clove garlic
2 tablespoon tomato paste
2 glasses dry white wine
water
salt as desired

Clean well ducklings, singe and truss them for roasting.

Arrange in a pan cut off parts such as wing tips, necks, etc.

Add butter, coarsley chopped onion and carrots, whole garlic and thyme. Place in oven until golden brown. Remove from oven and continue cooking over range. Skim fat and reserve.

Add tomato paste and stir for 2 minutes, sprinkle with a pinch of salt, 2 glasses of water and dry white wine. Heat to boiling then simmer until done occasionally skimming surface.

Peel an orange and cut rind into thin strips removing the white skin. Put rinds in a pot with a glass of water, heat to boiling for 3 minutes and drain. Squeeze peeled orange and reserve juice to be added to sauce. Peel remaining oranges and cut into segments with a sharpened knife thus removing the skins inbetween segments.

Rub ducklings with salt inside and outside and smear with reserved fat from cooking wing tips, necks etc., and roast in moderate to hot oven for 30 to 40 minutes or more, depending on taste. At fist arrange ducklings on legs for 10 minutes each side then turn them on the back. Frequently baste with liquid in pan. Remove from oven and transfer ducklings on a plate. Drain dripping in a cup and reserve it for other roasts.

Transfer sauce in pan where ducklings were cooked, heat to boiling for 3 minutes and strain.

Combine sugar with 2 tablespoons water and heat until sugar becomes brown, add vinegar and allow to boil until evaporated, pour strained sauce and simmer for 1 minute. Blend cornstarch with 2 tablespoons water and fold in sauce then allow to boil for 2 minutes longer.

Strain through cheesecloth or a fine mesh strainer. Pour sauce in a casserole, add reserved orange juice, rind strips, guava or orange jelly and liquor; stir and serve either separately or spread on ducklings previously cut into serving portions.

Heat orange segments for 1 minute and garnish ducklings.

To vary use stoned cherries or grapefruit segments instead of orange consequently changing liquor and jelly.

Serve preferably with crispy lettuce hearts placed in freezer just a few minutes before serving and seasoned with a little oil, salt and pepper and the juice of selected citrus.

BABY
LAMB
IN
CASSEROLE
CELIMONTANA

173

To serve 4 persons

2 lbs baby lamb meat
4 1/2 oz oil
2 cloves garlic
2 oz parsley
2 sprigs rosemary
1/2 teaspoon black pepper
Salt as desired
1 glass dry white wine
3 tablespoons vinegar
8 artichokes
8 mint leaves

Cut lamb meat into 1 inch cubes. Arrange in a pan with oil and brown for 10 minutes. Add salt and pepper, stir and sprinkle with white wine. Cover and cook over low heat for 20 minutes. Add finely chopped rosemary, garlic and parsley, stir for a few minutes then sprinkle with vinegar, allow to evaporate and serve at once.

While lamb is cooking, cut artichokes into eights, remove outer woody leaves and trim inner ones. Cook in pan with oil, salt and pepper. Remove from heat, arrange on serving platter and sprinkle with chopped mint leaves.

BREASTS
OF
CHICKEN
BIFFI
SCALA

To serve 4 persons

4 chicken breasts, medium sized
salt as desired
4 1/2 oz heavy cream
Bread crumbs
3 oz butter
3 sage leaves
1 scallion

2 oz meat gravy (Recipe N. 59)
1 dash nutmeg
1/2 lemon
1 lb small potatoes, roasted
3 oz cooked ham
1 oz parsley

Remove skins and bones from breasts except wing bone. Sprinkle with a few drops of cold water and pound thin. Slash breasts with a knife on both sides so as to make a lattice pattern. Rub with salt and arrange on a plate. Pour heavy cream all over breasts and let stand for 3 hours. Drain and reserve cream then roll in bread crumbs slightly pressing to make crumbs adhere. Melt 2 oz butter in pan, add scallion and sage leaves and cook breasts for 10 minutes on both sides or until golden brown. Remove and reserve in a warm place covered. Pour reserved cream in pan, add meat gravy and nutmeg and allow to boil for a few minutes. Strain through a fine mesh strainer and remove sage and scallion. Add remaining butter, lemon juice and whip until well blended.
Cut ham into thin strips and sauté for a few minutes.
Pour a little sauce on bottom of serving platter, arrange breasts and surround with roasted potatoes. Coat with remaining sauce, spread ham over and sprinkle with finely chopped parsley. Scald and serve.

VEAL
KIDNEY
PART
AU
GRATIN
EXCELSIOR

175

To serve 6 persons

3 lbs boneless veal kidney part	N. 74)
3 oz butter	5 1/2 oz sweetbreads
1 oz oil	4 1/2 oz mushrooms
1 small carrot	14 oz rice
1 celery stalk	2 oz grated cheese
1 small onion	Salt as desired
Rosemary or sage	1 pinch pepper
1 lb White Milk Sauce (Recipe	1 glass dry white wine

Remove inner skins, nervous and fatty tissues from meat and reserve. Split into halves, roll and fasten like any common roast. Rub with salt and pepper and arrange in a shallow casserole. Add 1 oz oil, 1 oz butter, diced carrot, celery and onion, rosemary and surround meat with chopped reserved skins, nervous and fatty tissues. Cover and begin cooking over low heat or oven. Turn meat every 15 minutes and baste with drippings in pan. Cook for about 2 hours or until done; to check, pierce meat with prongs of fork: if it is tender and no blood or moisture come out it means that meat is done.

Remove meat and leave casserole over heat until fat becomes almost transparent. Skim and strain it and reserve. Pour white wine in drippings in pan and allow to evaporate almost completely, add 2 glasses of water, boil for 10 minutes then strain and reserve gravy.

Cook or bake rice for 20 minutes and season with 1 oz melted butter. Butter a pan and spread rice evening it with a spoon. Cut veal into slices and arrange over rice.

While veal is cooking put cleaned sweetbreads in a casserole, cover with water, add vinegar, a pinch of salt and cook for 20 minutes.

Drain and cut into dice. Sauté sliced mushrooms in a skillet with 1 tablespoon butter then sprinkle with a little salt.

Add diced sweetbreads and stir for 2 minutes then fold in white milk sauce. Add half of reserved gravy, mix and coat meat. Sprinkle with grated cheese and a few drops of reserved skimmed fat. Bake until au gratin and serve well hot.

FLAMED BEEF FILLETS NERONE

To serve 4 persons

1 1/4 lb beef fillet
4 bay leaves
Salt as desired
4 tablespoons oil
1 clove garlic
1 pinch black pepper
1 pinch paprika
4 1/2 oz lean salt pork
2 tablespoons Cognac or brandy
Fried potatoes to serve 4 persons
4 Uncle Donald's Peppers (Recipe N. 183)

Remove skin and fat from fillet then cut into 1 inch cubes and marinate for a few hours with salt, 2 tablespoons oil, pepper, paprika, squeezed garlic and bay leaves halves.
Stir mixture occasionally. Fill skewers alternating diced fillet, salt pork squares and bay leaves. Heat 2 tablespoons oil in pan and brown prepared skewers for 10 minutes or as desired. Remove from heat and sprinkle with Cognac. Ignite and serve while blazing continues. Garnish with fried potatoes and Uncle Donald's Peppers.

IDEAL

VEAL

CHOPS

To serve 4 persons

4 veal chops, 1/2 lb each
3 oz butter
2 oz oil
Dredging flour
1/2 lb mushrooms
1 lb small potatoes
2 oz parsley
1 oz scallion
2 oz white truffles (optional)
salt as desired
1 lemon

Pare potatoes and roast them with 1 oz oil and 1 oz butter. Reserve in a warm place.
Finely chop parsley and scallion. Clean mushrooms, wash and cut into thin slices then sprinkle with lemon juice.
Cut truffles into thin slices.
Rub chops with salt and dredge with flour. Heat 1 oz oil and 1 oz butter in pan and brown chops for 5 minutes on each side.
Select a pan, preferably pyrexware, with a perfectly sealing lid. Butter it and spread half mushrooms evenly on bottom.
Sprinkle with a pinch of salt and spread chopped scallion and parsley. Arrange chops and surround with roasted potatoes.
Top with remaining mushrooms and sliced truffles and cover.
Place in oven for 15 minutes. Remove from oven and serve at once.

THE CLASSICAL SYLVANIA CHICKEN

178

To serve 4 persons

1 chicken, 2 1/2 lbs about	N. 59)	1 oz garlic
Dredging flour	4 mushroom caps medium	1/2 oz tarragon leaves
Salt and pepper	sized	4 1/2 oz tomato purée
2 bay leaves	1/2 lb rice	2 oz oil
1 glass Marsala or Port wine	3 oz butter	1 pinch Cayenne pepper
1 scallion	1 pinch paprika	1 glass Cognac or Brandy
1/2 pint heavy cream	4 lbs lobster	1 glass dry white wine
1/2 pint Meat Gravy (Recipe	1 oz parsley	1 lemon

Split chicken into quarters and remove as many bones as possible. Wash and pat dry. Rub with salt and pepper and dredge with flour. Melt 2 oz butter in a pan, arrange chicken, add bay leaves, allow to brown then sprinkle with Marsala or Port wine and allow to evaporate completely.

Add meat gravy, heavy cream and paprika, cover and cook over low heat for 1/2 hour. Blend 1 teaspoon butter with 1/2 teaspoon flour, fold in chicken sauce and cook for 2 minutes longer. Remove from heat and reserve in a warm place.

Cut live lobster tail into 1 inch pieces. Cut head into halves lengtwise, remove entrails and reserve them.

Heat oil in a casserole and arrange lobster pieces. Add salt and pepper constantly stirring until lobster begins to roast. Sprinkle with Cognac and let evaporate. Add chopped garlic, stir for a few minutes and pour white wine. Allow to evaporate then add tomato purée and a ladle of water.

Stir and cover and allow to cook for 30 minutes. Remove lobster pieces with skimmer, cool and remove meat from shell reserving head. Press reserved entrails through a sieve, add remaining butter, chopped parsley and tarragon, Cayenne pepper, and lemon juice. Mix well and fold in sauce. Take from heat immediately and return lobster pieces to its sauce. Cook rice for 20 minutes. Sauté mushroom caps in 1 tablespoon butter with scallion or garlic.

Arrange lobster heads in center of platter, surround with lobster meat. Place chicken all around and coat with a little of its sauce then top with mushroom caps. Pour chicken and lobster sauces into two separate gravy boats. Serve with cooked rice to be seasoned with either sauces or both as desired.

MUSHROOMS IN VINE LEAVES MIRAMARE

179

To serve 6 persons

1 1/2 lbs mushrooms
6 vine leaves
1 pinch salt
1 pinch pepper
1 pinch origan
2 cloves garlic
3 oz olive oil
1/2 glass white wine

Line bottom of a pan, preferably pyrexware, with well washed vine leaves. Sprinkle with white wine. Clean mushrooms and separate caps from stems. Cut stems into small dice and seson with a pinch of salt and pepper, origan and chopped garlic. Mix and fill mushroom caps with this mixture. Arrange caps neatly on vine leaves, sprinkle with oil, cover and bake in moderate oven for 15 minutes. Serve at once removing lid before guests.

EGGPLANT
TIMBALE
PARMESAN
FASHION

To serve 6 persons

3 lbs eggplants
1/2 lb oil
2 oz butter
1 lb Basil flavored tomato pulp (Recipe N. 63)
3 oz grated Parmesan cheese
3 oz Mozzarella or Swiss cheese
1 oz fresh basil

Peel eggplants and cut into half inch slices lenghtwise.
Heat oil in a pan and fry eggplants 3 minutes on both sides.
Drain on a grate and sprinkle with a little salt.
Oil a baking pan and arrange a first layer of fried eggplants and spread a layer of tomato pulp, sprinkle with two chopped basil leaves and grated Parmesan cheese and dot with diced Mozzarella or Swiss cheese. Continue until eggplants have been used. Top with a layer of tomato pulp, sprinkle with cheese and dot with butter. Bake in moderate oven for 15 minutes and serve at once.
To vary, use meat gravy (Recipe N. 59) instead of basil flavored tomato pulp.

BAKED
STUFFED
ONIONS
BERMUDA

To serve 6 persons

12 small onions
1/2 lb fresh bread crumbs
1 1/2 pint dairy fresh milk
3 eggs
2 oz grated cheese
2 oz raisins
Salt and pepper
2 oz butter
1 dash nutmeg

Peel onions and boil whole in one quart water and 1/2 oz salt for 10 minutes. Drain and allow to cool. Cut a half inch slice on stem side and scoop out inside pulp with a spoon being careful not to break shell. Chop pulp and brown for a few minutes in a pan with 1 oz melted butter. Soak bread crumbs in 1/2 pint milk for 5 minutes, squeeze, chop and add to browned onion. Wash raisins and add to mixture together with a pinch of salt, pepper and grated cheese. Thoroughly mix and fill onions with mixture. Smear a pan with remaining butter and arrange onions. Pan must be large enough to contain all stuffed onions on one layer. Heat remaining milk to boiling.
Combine eggs in a bowl with a pinch of salt and nutmeg and pour boiling milk over eggs beating for 1 minute. Spread egg mixture over onions and bake in moderate oven in bain marie for 1/2 hour. Serve either hot, lukewarm or cold.

ZUCCHINI AU GRATIN THERMIDOR

To serve 6 persons

6 zucchini, medium sized
1/2 lb sweetbreads
1 oz onions
1 oz parsley
2 oz grated cheese
3 egg yolks
5 1/2 oz mushrooms
5 1/2 oz ripe tomatoes
1/2 lb heavy cream
salt as desired
3 oz butter
1 pinch pepper

Peel and wash zucchini then boil in one quart water for 5 minutes with 2 teaspoon salt. Drain and allow to cool.

Cut into halves lengthwise and scoop out inside pulp without breaking shell. Precook sweetbreads in water and chop together with onions and zucchini pulp. Add chopped parsley, egg yolks and half grated cheese. Mix until well blended.

Cut mushrooms into thin slices. Peel tomatoes and coarsely chop them. Melt 1 oz butter in a skillet add mushrooms and brown for 5 minutes then add tomatoes, a pinch of salt and pepper. Stir to combine ingredients and fill reserved zucchini pods with this mixture. Top with sweetbreads mixture. Butter a baking pan and pour slightly salted heavy cream. Arrange zucchini and sprinkle with remaining grated cheese and melted butter. Bake for 20 minutes or until golden brown.

THE
APPETIZING
PEPPERS
OF
UNCLE DONALD

To serve 6 persons

6 large peppers
3 medium sized tomatoes
3 cloves garlic
1 pinch origan
6 anchovies
3 oz olive oil
1 pinch salt
1 teaspoon sugar

Choose large, fleshy red and yellow peppers. Cut into halves lengthwise, remove seeds and wash. Oil a pan large enough to contain all pepper halves on one layer. Arrange peppers hollow side up. Peel ripe tomatoes, squeeze out seeds, chop and fill peppers. Slice garlic cloves and cut anchovies into pieces then divide garlic and anchovies in equal amounts on each pepper. Combine sugar, origan and a pinch of salt and sprinkle over peppers. Sprinkle with remaining oil and bake in moderate oven for 20 minutes or until peppers collapse on pan bottom. Serve either hot or cold and use as hours d'oeuvre or to garnish meat and poultry.

RED CABBAGE FLAVORED WITH ANTIGUA SPICES

To serve 6 persons

3 lbs red cabbage
4 1/2 oz butter or margarine
1 oz brown sugar
2 oz onions
6 cloves
1 pinch powdered cinnamon
2 bay leaves
3 apples
2 oz red vinegar
1/2 oz salt
1 pinch pepper
1 oz cornstarch or arrowroot

Clean red cabbage and cut into strips as thin as possible.
Combine butter and chopped onions in a casserole and as soon as it becomes transparent add cabbage, salt, pared and sliced apples, a glass of water, bay leaves, sugar and cloves. Cover and cook for 45 minutes frequently stirring.
Uncover if sauce is too liquid at the end of cooking, and simmer until thickened. Combine cornstarch, pepper, cinnamon and vinegar in a bowl, mix until well blended and pour over cabbage. Stir and cook 5 minutes longer. Excellent especially with fat meats, ducks, pork, etc.

184

ASPARAGUS WITH EGGS AND CHEESE MILAN FASHION

To serve 6 persons

3 lbs asparagus
12 eggs
6 1/2 oz butter
4 1/2 oz grated Parmesan or
Swiss cheese
2 oz salt
4 quarts water

Scrap asparagus and repeatedly wash in cold water to remove any traces of earth. Tie them up into six bundles with a thin thread. Trim asparagus on the woody side to equalize length. Heat water with salt to boiling then dip asparagus and cook for 15 minutes being careful not to overcook. As tips become tender, remove and drain.
Arrange asparagus on six individual plates and sprinkle tips with grated cheese. Melt 1 oz butter in a skillet and allow to brown then break two eggs and cook as desired.
Arrange shirred eggs over asparagus and sprinkle with melted butter remained in skillet. Repeat operation for all portions.
To vary, precook asparagus as above and dip in foamy sauce (Recipe N. 75) or use to garnish any meat dish.

MINT FLAVORED SPRING CARROTS

To serve 6 persons

2 lbs spring carrots
3 oz butter
1 teaspoon sugar
1 teaspoon salt
1 pinch pepper
12 mint leaves

Scrap carrots accurately and remove any blak spot.
Wash and cut into slices as thin as possible. Use a vegetable slicer for best results. Put sliced carrots in a pan, add 2 glasses water, butter, sugar, salt and pepper. Cover and cook for about 1/2 hour or until done.
Sprinkle with chopped mint leaves and stir until sauce is thickened. If too liquid increase heat and cook until evaporated.

SPINACH
BALLS
CASTELLANA

To serve 6 persons

1 lb creamed cottage cheese or
ricotta
2 lbs spinach
1 teaspoon salt
1 pinch pepper
1 dash nutmeg
2 egg yolks
2 whole eggs
3 oz grated Swiss cheese
3 oz butter
Dredging flour

Clean and wash spinach. Boil and drain then allow to cool.
Squeeze out excess water and combine in a bowl with
creamed cottage cheese, mix for a while then force through
food chopper using a coarse attachment. Return to bowl,
add salt as necessary, pepper, nutmeg and eggs. Blend well
with a spatula and split mixture into balls large as a walnut.
Heat a broad pan with water enough to cover a standing egg
and add salt as necessary (1 teaspoon salt is needed for each
quart water). Heat water to boiling and then simmer.
Dredge balls with flour and drop in water cooking them for
5 minutes gradually, keeping water below boiling point.
Remove with skimmer and place delicately on a hot plate.
Sprinkle with grated cheese and browned butter.

STUFFED
EGGPLANTS
PAOLO
MONETTI

To serve 6 persons

6 small eggplants
5 1/2 oz oil
4 tablespoons grated cheese
2 peppers
3 tomatoes
1/2 lb fresh bread crumbs
2 oz butter
2 oz parsley
6 anchovies

Peel eggplants, cut into halves lengthwise and fry in hot oil for 5 minutes. Allow to cool then scoop out inside pulp with a spoon leaving a half inch pod to be refilled.
Combine pulp, 2 tablespoons oil and 2 tablespoons grated cheese in a bowl and work with a spatula until well blended and creamy. Clean peppers and cut into strips then fry in 1 tablespoon oil. Peel tomatoes and cut into dice.
Sauté together with peppers for 2 minutes adding a pinch of salt. Remove from heat and add anchovies cut into bits.
Delicately stir to combine. Fill eggplants with peppers mixture and coat surface with prepared eggplant pulp mixture.
Combine remaining grated cheese with bread crumbs and fold in eggplants delicately. Butter a baking pan, arrange eggplants and sprinkle with remaining oil. Bake in oven until golden brown. Finely chop parsley leaves and sprinkle over eggplants when taken from oven. Serve either hot or cold.

BELGIAN ENDIVE AU GRATIN

To serve 6 persons

12 Belgian endive pieces
2 oz butter
1/2 lb heavy cream
2 scallions
3 oz Swiss cheese
salt to taste
1 dash nutmeg
1 ladle beef stock or extract
broth

Combine 1 oz butter, chopped scallions, well washed endive, a pinch of salt, beef stock or water with half teaspoon beef extract in a pan. Cover and cook slowly for 1/2 hour.
Add water during cooking if endives become too dry.
Add heavy cream and nutmeg. Continue cooking for another 15 minutes or until tender. Uncover and dot with diced Swiss cheese and remaining butter. Place in hot oven until cheese melts through endives and serve to garnish any meat dish.
To vary use meat gravy (Recipe N. 59) instead of heavy cream and follow same procedure.

STRING BEANS AU GRATIN LUCILLA

To serve 6 persons

2 lbs string beans
2 oz butter
2 oz grated cheese
2 eggs
1 oz onion
3 oz heavy cream
1 1/2 oz salt
1 pinch pepper
1 dash nutmeg

Boil cleaned string beans in a pot with 4 quarts water and salt for about 15 minutes until tender but not completely done. Drain in a colander. Combine 1 oz butter and chopped onion in a pan. Heat for 2 minutes without browning then add beans, pepper and nutmeg. Stir for 2 minutes and transfer in a buttered pan. Slightly beat eggs and blend in cream and grated cheese. Pour mixture over beans and bake in bain-marie until au gratin.

GARDEN
PEAS
FRENCH
STYLE

To serve 6 persons

2 lbs shelled fresh peas
12 spring onions, small
2 Boston lettuce
3 oz butter
1/2 salt
1 teaspoon sugar
1 pinch pepper

In a casserole, combine well washed peas, spring onions lettuce hearts cut into strips, butter, salt, pepper and sugar. Pour water to cover peas, cover and simmer for 1/2 hour. Uncover and continue cooking over high heat if sauce is too liquid.

191

ARTICHOKE PIE A LA MODERNA

To serve 6 persons

12 artichokes
4 1/2 oz butter
1 lemon
1/2 lb White Milk Sauce
(Recipe N. 74)
1/2 lb mushrooms
3 oz grated Parmesan or Swiss
cheese
3 tablespoons meat gravy
(Recipe N. 59)
salt to taste
1 pinch pepper
4 1/2 oz flour

Clean artichokes, remove outer leaves, trim woody parts and cut into thin slices. Put in a pan with 2 oz butter a pinch of salt and pepper and lemon juice. Cook covered until tender. Artichockes must be stewed without browning or roasting. Add a little water if during cooking they turn out too dry. 10 minutes after add sliced mushrooms and cook for 5 minutes longer. Add white milk sauce, meat gravy, grated cheese and stir well.
Butter a round baking pan, 10-inch in diameter.
Combine flour and 2 oz butter, add some water and prepare a dough kneading for a few minutes. Roll out thin and line baking pan. Pour in prepared artichoke mixture and fold dough to cover. Press edges to seal and prick surface with prongs of fork. Bake in moderate oven for 1/2 hour or until golden brown. Allow to become lukewarm before serving.

PUMPKIN
PUDDING
BALTIMORE

To serve 6 persons

2 lbs pumpkin
2 oz butter
4 eggs
salt as desired
1 pinch pepper
1 pinch powdered cinnamon
1 teaspoon sugar
Dredging flour
1/2 lb white milk sauce
(Recipe N. 74)

Remove rind and seeds from a well ripe pumpkin.
Cut into slices as thin as possible. Arrange slices in a casserole with 1 oz butter, a little salt and half glass of water. Cover and cook for 20 minutes. Press through a sieve or force through food chopper.
In the same casserole where pumpkin was cooked, melt 1 oz butter and add pumpkin purée. Stir with a spatula constantly until water evaporates and purée is thickened.
Remove from heat, add white milk sauce, pepper, sugar, cinnamon and constantly stirring fold in eggs one by one.
Butter a mold and dredge well with flour, pour in prepared mixture and bake in oven in bain-marie until crust is hard. Unmold and coat with either sauces from recipes N. 68, 59 and 57.

CAULIFLOWER QUEEN OF THE BAHAMAS

To serve 6 persons

3 lbs cauliflower
4 1/2 oz butter
2 oz boiled ham
2 eggs
1 oz bread crumbs
2 oz parsley
salt as desired
1 pinch pepper

Boil cauliflower in 2 quarts water and 2 teaspoons salt.
Drain and cut into small pieces disposing of stem.
Hard cook eggs (8 minutes), remove shells and chop. Chop ham, and parsley leaves. Melt 2 oz butter in a pan and add cauliflower. Delicately stir until brown. Sprinkle with chopped parsley, eggs and pepper. Put remaining butter in a pan together with chopped ham and bread crumbs, allow to brown for 2 minutes and spread over cauliflower.
Scald and serve. Excellent with meats and particulary suggested with pork meats.

CREAMED
BROCCOLI,
FOAMY
SAUCE

To serve 6 persons

2 lbs fresh or frozen broccoli
2 oz butter
2 teaspoons salt
1 pinch pepper
1/2 lb Foamy Sauce (Recipe
N. 75)

Heat 2 quarts salted water to boiling and drop broccoli.
Allow to cook for 15 minutes. Drain and press through a
sieve to make a purée. Brown butter in a pan and add
broccoli purée stirring with a spoon until water is
evaporated then sprinkle with pepper. Transfer purée in a
cocotte and cover with Foamy Sauce.
To vary, serve whole cooked broccoli with sauce.

BRUSSELS SPROUTS WITH BACON

To serve 6 persons
2 lbs Brussels sprouts
4 1/2 oz bacon strips
salt to taste
1 pinch pepper
1 dash nutmeg
1 teaspoon sugar

Heat 3 quarts water to boiling with 1 oz salt then drop sprouts. Cook for 20 minutes and drain.
Slightly sauté bacon in a pan and add sprouts, pepper, sugar and nutmeg. Delicately stir, cover and stew for 10 minutes to allow sprouts to gain flavor. Serve at once.

BRAISED CELERY IN MEAT GRAVY

To serve 6 persons

2 lbs celery hearts
2 oz carrots
2 oz onions
3 oz salt pork
5 pepper grains
Water or broth
salt as desired
1/2 lb Meat Gravy (Recipe N.
59)

Clean and wash celery, boil for 5 minutes and drain.
Cut salt pork into thin strips and arrange on bottom of casserole together with sliced onions, sliced carrots and pepper grains. Arrange celery as well, add salt and pour water or broth to the level of celery. Cover and heat to boiling. Remove and bake in oven for 1 hour. Take from oven, allow to cool and cut celery into 2 inch pieces.
Return to pan coat with meat gravy and bake until surface is glazed. Serve hot.

BAKED STUFFED TOMATOES WITH RICE CREOLE

To serve 6 to 12 persons

14 medium sized tomatoes
1/2 lb rice
salt as desired
1 pinch pepper
1 oz mint leaves or basil
1 oz onions
1 teaspoon sugar
3 oz oil
2 oz butter

Select 12 ripe tomatoes and cut tops crosswise at stem ends at 3/4 of their length. Save slice to act as lid.
Scoop out center pulp delicately without breaking shell.
Cook rice in 1 quart water and 1 teaspoon salt for 15 minutes. Drain and season with 1 oz butter and finely chopped basil or mint leaves. Fill tomatoes with rice and top with reserved slices. Arrange in buttered baking pan.
Press pulp through a sieve together with two remaining tomatoes. Sauté chopped onions in a skillet with oil without browning, add sifted tomato pulp, a pinch of salt, sugar and pepper and heat to boiling. Pour sauce over tomatoes and bake in moderate oven for 20 minutes. Serve either hot or cold. To vary, use small pastas instead of rice.

WATERCRESS PUREE NIAGARA

To serve 6 persons

2 lbs watercress
1 lb potatoes
2 oz heavy cream
2 oz butter
1 oz salt
1 pinch pepper
1 dash nutmeg

Pour 3 quarts water and 1 oz salt in a pot. Heat to boiling and add pared potatoes cut into 1/2 inch slices. Boil for 10 minutes and add watercress previously cleaned and washed. Allow to cook for 10 minutes longer, drain and press both potatoes and watercress through a sieve or food chopper.
Transfer purée in a casserole, reheat and add butter constantly stirring for 3 minutes. Add pepper, nutmeg and cream.
Stir for another minute and serve. Particularly suggested with veal or lamb meats.

ALBA PEARLS WITH CHAMPAGNE

To serve 6 to 12 persons

1 lb white truffles
2 oz butter
1 sprig sage
1/2 bottle Champagne
1 pinch salt
1 pinch pepper

Clean truffles with a brush and water. Melt butter with the sprig of sage in a casserole, preferably pyrexware and hermetically sealing. As soon as sage flavor is smelt, remove sprig and add truffles, salt and pepper and allow to brown for 3 minutes. Pour Champagne, cover and cook for 20 minutes. Serve at once removing lid in front of guests so as to enjoy full flavor.

200

SOUFFLEED
POTATOES

To serve 6 persons

6 medium sized potatoes
2 pints oil or other frying fats
1 pinch salt

Pare potatoes and wash, then dry them on a napkin. Cut lengthwise into thin slices and pat further dry. Fry in not too hot deep oil or fat for 5 minutes or until potatoes float. Be sure to keep oil below frying point for best results. As potatoes float, make a whirlpool with skimmer and fry 2 minutes longer then remove and drain on a grate.
Repeat operation until all potatoes have been used.
Heat oil well and dip potatoes again but gradually. Shake pan to induce a whrilpool or waving motion in oil. When potatoes begin to swell, turn with skimmer until golden brown, remove and return on grate to drain.
Sprinkle with salt and serve with steaks.

PINEAPPLE GLAZED SWEETPOTATOES

To serve 6 persons

6 sweetpotatoes
1 small pineapple
4 1/2 oz sugar
1 lb pineapple juice
2 oz butter

Pare potatoes and cut into 1/2 inch thick slices. Clean and core pineapple; cut into segments lengthwise to match potatoes. Arrange potato and pineapple slices in baking pan alternated. Combine sugar, pineapple juice and butter in a pot, heat to boiling for 2 minutes and sprinkle in pan. Bake in moderate oven for 1 hour frequently basting with liquid in pan. When cooking is finished, sauce must be thickened. If this is not the case, remove from oven and heat on range until thickened.

BROWNED SWEETPOTATOES O'BRIEN

To serve 6 persons

6 medium sized potatoes
1 green pepper
1 red pepper
1 spring or small onion
4 1/2 oz oil

Pare potatoes and cut into 1/2 inch cubes. Heat half oil in a pan and brown potatoes for 15 minutes.
Clean pepper, remove seeds and cut into dice to match potatoes. Heat remaining oil and sauté chopped onion for 2 minutes then add peppers, stir and cook for 5 minutes. Delicately fold with potatoes and allow to cook for 5 minutes longer. Serve at once.

POTATOES AU GRATIN DAUPHINOIS

To serve 6 persons

6 medium sized potatoes
2 pints milk
2 oz butter
1 teaspoon salt
1 pinch pepper
1 clove garlic
3 oz grated Swiss Cheese
4 1/2 oz heavy cream

Pare potatoes and cut into thin slices. Combine sliced potatoes in a pot with milk, 1 oz butter, salt and pepper and simmer for 10 minutes.
Squeeze garlic and rub a pan closely. Pour potato mixture, cover with cream, dust with grated Swiss cheese and dot with remaining butter. Bake in low oven for 1 hour about.

POTATO
PANCAKES

2 medium sized potatoes
1 small onion
1 tablespoon flour
1 tablespoon baking powder
1 egg
1 pinch salt
1 pinch pepper
Oil or bacon fat
2 tablespoons heavy cream

Peel onion and pare potatoes. Force them through food
chopper and combine in a bowl with salt, pepper, flour and
egg previously beaten with cream.
Add baking powder and thoroughly mix to blend
ingredients.
Heat enough fat or oil in pan, form with spoon small
pancakes and fry in hot fat for a few minutes or until
golden brown. Drain on a grate and serve at once.
Excellent with apple sauce, sour cream, bilberry sauce, meat
gravy or as garnishment for various meat dishes.

DELICIOUS POTATO CROQUETTES

4 medium sized potatoes
3 eggs
2 oz butter
salt as desired
1 pinch pepper
1 dash nutmeg
2 oz mixed celery, carrots and
chives
Bread crumbs
oil or fat for frying.

Pare potatoes and cut into halves. Cook them in a casserole with 1 quart water and 1 teaspoon salt. 20 minutes to 1/2 hour will be necessary, depending on potatoes used.
Be careful in any case to remove them undercooked. Drain and press through a sieve or potato ricer to make a purée.
Return to casserole, reheat constantly stirring for 5 minutes. Take from heat and add pepper, nutmeg and two egg yolks reserving whites. Chop celery, carrots and chives very finely and sauté in a skillet with butter without browning. Add to purée and mix. Place purée on table or board and shape into balls or any other desired shape. Dredge with flour and dip in slightly beaten egg yolk and whites. Remove excess egg and roll in bread crumbs.
Gently press croquettes so that crumbs adhere. Fry in hot deep oil or fat until golden brown.

WESTERN   SUN   SALAD

1 chicory
1 lettuce
1 escarole
1 pepper
1 pinch chopped garlic
3 oz Gorgonzola or Roquefort

Cut all vegetables into thin strips. Mince cheese and mix to vegetables. Sprinkle with finely chopped garlic.

CHICKEN
AND MELON
SALAD

1/2 lb boiled or roast chicken
1 lb melon
6 lettuce leaves

Dice chicken and melon. Mix together and arrange on lettuce leaves.

PAPAYA AND SWISS CHEESE

ST. LUCIA

1 lb papaya
4 1/2 oz Swiss Cheese
6 cherries
6 mint leaves
1 lemon
1 teaspoon sugar

Cut papaya and swiss cheese into slices. Combine in a bowl, stud with cherries, sprinkle with coarsely chopped mint leaves, sugar and lemon juice.

CAESAR SALAD

2 lettuce
1 tablespoon grated cheese
1 boiled egg (3 minutes)
2 anchovy fillets
2 toasts
1 clove garlic
2 tablespoons Vinegar
Dressing (Recipe N. 234)

Cut lettuce into thin strips and sprinkle with grated cheese. Rub toast with garlic, remove crusts, cut into half inch cubes and add to lettuce. Separately blend mashed anchovies with boiled egg add Vinegar dressing and continue stirring until well blended. Spread on salad and mix well before serving.

210

CABBAGE

SALAD

2 lbs cabbage
1/2 lb peppers
2 oz onions

Chop cabbage as finely as possible, cut peppers into thin
strips. Soak finely sliced onions in salted water for one
hour. Combine all ingredients together, mix well and season
with desired dressing.

AVOCADO, TOMATO AND WATERCRESS

2 avocados
2 tomatoes
1/2 lb watercress

Cut avocado into segments and arrange in center of salad bowl. Surround with sliced tomatoes and garnish with watercress. Season with desired dressing.

ITALIAN

SALAD

2 lettuce
3 oz mushrooms
2 truffles, Medium sized
Vinegar Dressing (Recipe N.
234)

Arrange lettuce hearts on a plate broadening leaves. Top
with mushrooms and finely sliced truffles. Season with
vinegar dressing.

AVOCADO
GRAPEFRUIT
AND
PINEAPPLE

Cut into a same size an equal amount of avocado, grapefruit and pineapple. Garnish with lettuce leaves.

LETTUCE
HEARTS,
GRAPEFRUIT
AND
ALMONDS

Top lettuce hearts with grapefruit segments and sprinkle with finely shredded sweet toasted almonds.

AVOCADO

ORANGE

AND

CELERY

2 avocados
3 oranges
1 celery

Cut avocado into slices. Cut orange into segments. Cut celery heart into thin strips. Mix and garnish with celery stalks.

216

TOMATOES, BANANAS, GRAPEFRUIT AND CHERRIES

Cut tomatoes into segments. Slice bananas. Cut grapefruit into segments. Stone cherries and cut into halves. Mix bananas and grapefruit, crown with tomatoes and top center with cherries.

PEACHES,
CARROTS
AND
LETTUCE

Cut peaches into halves and remove stones. Arrange peach halves on lettuce leaves top with grated carrots and sprinkle with chopped peanuts.

APPLES, CELERY AND ALMONDS

Dice celery and apples. Sprinkle with sweet toasted almonds finely sliced.

LETTUCE
SALAD
AND
ORANGE

Cut lettuce hearts into halves, top with orange segments and sprinkle with a pinch of finely chopped parsley leaves.

CUCUMBER
SALAD

Peel and cut cucumbers into thin slices. Soak in salted water for 1/2 hour. Squeeze and season with heavy cream, lemon juice, paprika and chopped chives.

MUSHROOMS

AND

POTATOES

Slice boiled potatoes. Cut mushrooms into thin slices. Chop green olives and parsley. Combine all ingredients and mix, add pepper, lemon juice top with heavy cream and a little mayonnaise.

CARROT

SALAD

Top lettuce hearts with grated carrots. Season with mayonnaise and dot with grape berries halves without seeds.

WALDORF
SALAD

Select finest lettuce leaves and put in a bowl. Top with celery hearts and apples cut into dice. Season with mayonnaise and garnish with walnut kernels.

SAUCE
MAYONNAISE

6 egg yolks
1 teaspoon salt
1 pinch white pepper
4 lemons
1 pint oil
4 tablespoons white winegar
1/2 tablespoon powdered mustard
1/2 teaspoon sugar (optional)

For best results use any concave container, large enough to allow easy blending of ingredients and a flexible whip or an electric mixer.

Combine egg yolks, salt, white pepper, lemon juice and powdered mustard. Begin whipping for 3 minutes with regular strokes. Pour oil drop after drop, keeping on whipping. Stop pouring oil during whipping pauses.

If mayonnaise becomes too thick in the course of preparation, add a few drops of vinegar. Sprinkle half tablespoon cold water and finish whipping adding all or remaining vinegar. The addition of cold water is necessary to prevent ingredients from dividing. If mayonnaise is not readily used, store it in a porcelain or glass container in a cool place but do not refrigerate. Wishing a sweeter taste, add sugar in the beginning.

Use mayonnaise plain or blended with any other sweet or piquant dressings or mixed with other sauces such as katchup, chili, etc.

BLUE
CHEESE
DRESSING

1/2 lb blue cheese
1/2 oz onion
2 oz vinegar
3 oz oil
3 oz Sauce Mayonnaise
(Recipe N. 235)
1 pinch paprika or pepper

236

Combine chopped blue cheese, finely minced onion, oil, vinegar, mayonnaise, paprika or pepper in a bowl. Work with a fork or whip until blended and serve on salads.

TARTAR SAUCE

1 lb Sauce Mayonnaise
(Recipe N. 235)
2 oz gherkins in vinegar
1 oz capers
1 oz parsley
1/2 oz tarragon leaves
1 oz scallions or onions
2 hard cooked eggs
2 tablespoons vinegar
(preferably tarragon flavored)

Clean onions or scallions, select parsley and tarragon leaves only and wash thoroughly in fresh water. Finely chop gherkins, capers, parsley, tarragon, scallions or onions.
Combine with mayonnaise, add vinegar and minced eggs, mix well until blended and serve.
Suggested with sea food, fish or cold meats.

237

GARLIC
FLAVORED
MAYONNAISE

1 lb Sauce Mayonnaise
(Recipe N. 235)
2 oz garlic
3 lemons
2 hard cooked egg yolks
salt to taste

Pound garlic in a mortar together with salt and egg yolks
until fluffy or use an electric mixer. Add lemon juice and
blend in with mayonnaise. Use as salad dressing or with fish.

THOUSAND

ISLANDS

DRESSING

1/2 lb Sauce Mayonnaise
(Recipe N. 235)
1 orange
1 lemon
1/2 oz onion
1 oz parsley
2 oz roasted red peppers
2 oz stoned green olives
1 teaspoon Worcestershire
sauce

Chop onion, parsley, peppers and olives very finely.
Blend in with orange juice, lemon juice, Worcestershire
sauce and mayonnaise.

RUSSIAN
DRESSING

1/2 lb Sauce Mayonnaise
(Recipe N. 235)
1 red pepper
1 green pepper
1/2 oz onion
4 1/2 oz Tomato Katchup
2 oz oil
2 oz vinegar
1 pinch paprika
2 oz smoked salmon
(optional)

Finely chop peppers and onion. Combine in a salad bowl
with oil, vinegar, paprika, tomato katchup, mayonnaise and
diced smoked salmon. Mix well until blended and serve.

PIQUANT
DRESSING
FOR BEANS
AND
CHICK PEAS

To serve 6 persons

1 oz tuna fish in oil
1 oz anchovies
1 oz onions
1 clove garlic
2 oz oil
1 oz vinegar
1 pinch pepper
1 oz parsley or tarragon leaves
Basil to taste

Combine all ingredients and chop as finely as possible. Add oil and vinegar. Mix well and season beans or chick peas at least one hour before serving.

LAS VEGAS
DRESSING

To serve 12 persons

2 oz parsley
1 oz capers
1 oz anchovies
1 oz scallion
1 teaspoon mustard
2 lemons
2 hard cooked eggs
1 lb Sauce Mayonnaise
(Recipe N. 235)

Finely chop parsley, capers, anchovies, scallion and eggs.
Put in a bowl add mustard and blend in lemon juice.
Combine with mayonnaise and mix until well blended.
Serve with sea food as well as with poultry or game salads.

WALNUT
SAUCE
FOR
BOILED FISH

To serve 6 persons

1/2 lb heavy cream
1 oz rasped horseradish
2 lemons
1 pinch salt
4 1/2 oz shelled walnuts
1 pinch paprika

Chop walnuts as finely as possible. Combine with cream and
lemon juice, add salt, paprika and rasped horseradish.
Mix well with a whip until blended and serve.

PAPRIKA
DRESSING

To serve 6 persons

1 oz sweet paprika
1/2 lb heavy cream
1 oz chives
3 lemons
1 pinch salt
1 pinch pepper
2 oz tomato katchup

Combine heavy cream, tomato katchup, lemon juice, minced chives, salt, pepper and paprika, the latter previously diluted into two tablespoons hot water. Beat with a whip for a few minutes and serve on lobster, shrimps and sea food in general.

...ersons
...s oil
...ce
...een pepper
1 clove garlic
Few drops Tabasco
1 teaspoon Worcestershire
Sauce
3 teaspoons tomato katchup

Squeeze garlic and rub a salad bowl. Combine all ingredients, mix well and serve chilled.

YOGHOURT

DRESSING

1/2 lb plain yoghourt
2 lemons, juice
Paprika and salt to taste

Blend all ingredients in a mixer. Ideal to season vegetable and fruit salads.
Use orange juice, grapefruit juice or lime juice instead of lemon to season fruit salads.
Add grated cheese to taste, such as Gorgonzola, blue cheese, Parmesan cheese, Roquefort to serve with vegetable salads.

CHOCOLATE
SOUFFLE'

To serve 6 persons

1/2 pint milk
2 oz cocoa
2 oz sugar
2 oz butter
2 oz flour
3 eggs
1/2 pint heavy cream

Heat to boiling milk with sugar and cocoa. Separately blend butter and flour and shape into a ball. As milk boils, drop in prepared ball and stir with a spatula until creamy. Three minutes will be necessary. Remove from heat and allow to become lukewarm. Separate egg yolks and reserve whites in refrigerator. Add egg yolks to milk mixture constantly stirring for 2 or 3 minutes.

Butter individual ovenproof porcelain ramekins or a large one. Sprinkle sugar to coat butter completely. Stiffly beat reserved egg whites with a pinch of salt and a few drops of lemon juice. Fold into milk mixture, pour in ramekins and bake in moderate oven. 12 minutes baking will be necessary for individual portions whereas 20 minutes baking time are required if a single mold is used.

Take from heat and serve at once with sweetened whipped cream topping or plain whipped cream dusted with vanilla sugar.

To vary taste, use vanilla instead of cocoa. Heat milk to boiling with a pinch vanilla or a vanilla pod and follow same procedure.

Fresh fruits may also be used adding them before beaten egg whites. Or even better use candied fruit. Fruit soufflés are best accompanied by their corresponding sauces, that is cherry soufflé with cherry sauce etc.

Fruit sauces are made by diluting jellies or jams with water or sirups. Wishing to prepare home made fresh sauces, boil desired fruit with an equal amount of sugar for 10 minutes.

Strain through a sieve, return to pot and continue boiling to the desired consistency. Anyway, sauces should be served hot.

FRITTERS
VALLE
OMBROSA

To serve 6 persons

1 lb flour
2 whole eggs
3 egg yolks
3 oz powdered sugar
2 oz butter
1/2 teaspoon vanilla
1 glass Madeira or Marsala wine

Combine all ingredients on pastry board and knead until dough is satiny smooth or use a pastry blender. Cover dough with a napkin and let stand for one hour about.
Roll out 1/4 inch thin. Cut pastry into triangles, rectangles or any other desired shape using a pastry wheel. Heat fat or oil in a pan and dip pastry little at a time.
Fry until golden brown, remove with skimmer and drain on a grate or absorbent paper. Dust with vanilla sugar and serve at once. If desired serve fritters with vanilla sauce or an eggnog or a vanilla ice cream.

PIE
PASTRY
SHELL

1/2 lb flour
4 1/2 oz sugar
1 egg
5 1/2 oz butter
1/2 grated lemon or orange
rind

This simple pie pastry can be easily and quickly made and is the basis for the preparation of cream pies, fresh or canned fruit pies, jam pies, etc.
Combine all ingredients in pastry blender or on board.
Knead until dough is homogeneous.

Jam Pie

Roll out dough 1/4 inch thick. Line mold or pie pan with pastry and trim edges evenly. Fill with selected jam until 1/2 inch thick. Cut remaining pastry into 1/4 inch wide strips using a pastry wheel and arrange over jam in a lattice pattern. Press excess pastry together on the rim with prongs of fork to make an upright edge. Bake in moderate oven for 20 minutes.

Fresh Fruit Pie

Roll out dough as in previous recipe and line mold or piepan.
Prebake bottom crust until golden brown. Remove from oven and arrange fresh fruit: strawberries, pared and sliced apples and pears, bananas cut into slices crosswise, stoned cherries, peach halves, pineapple slices, etc. If desired use canned instead of fresh fruit. Top with fruit jelly made as follows:
Press canned apricots through a sieve. Weigh strained pulp and juice and put it in a casserole adding an equal amount of sugar. Heat to boiling then skim surface and allow to cook for 10 minutes or a little longer. To test if jelly is ready, take one tablespoon of cooking jelly and transfer it on a cold plate, if jelly hardens within a short time it means that it is ready. Brush with hot jelly the fruit in pie, cool and serve.
Store remaining jelly in a jar and place in refrigerator for a next occasion.

Cream Pie

Line pie pan as for previous recipes, prebake bottom crust and fill with cream prepared as follows.
4 1/2 oz sugar
4 egg yolks
1/2 pint milk
1/2 teaspoon vanilla
1/2 oz cornstarch
Heat milk to boiling. Combine remaining ingredients in a mixing bowl and whip until blended. Pour boiled milk gradually constantly stirring. Reheat mixture keeping on stirring. As boiling is resumed pour cream in pie. Cool and serve.
To vary, pour cream in pie and dust surface with sugar.
Bake in moderate oven until crust is golden brown. Cream may be further flavored with Maraschino, Kirsh, Curaçao, Grand Marnier, or with the addition of shredded fruits after removing from oven.

CARAMEL
CUSTARD

To serve 6 persons

1/2 lb sugar
1 pint milk
1 lemon rind
4 eggs

Put 3 1/2 oz sugar in a small pot, add half glass water and heat until sugar is golden brown. Remove from heat and distribute caramel into six individual molds. Heat milk to boiling adding a few pieces of lemon rind, yellow part only.

Combine eggs and remaining sugar in a bowl and whip for 2 minutes. Add boiling milk to egg mixture and stir until well blended. Remove lemon rinds and fill molds.

Bake in moderate oven in bain-marie for 40 minutes. Take from oven and allow to cool. Unmold and serve with small pastry or cookies.

To vary, use orange rind or a pinch vanilla, or one tablespoon cocoa instead of lemon. If desired prepare custards in ovenproof molds and serve without unmolding.

FLUFFY TAPIOCA PUDDING

To serve 6 persons

1 pint milk
4 1/2 oz tapioca
3 oz sugar
4 eggs, separated
1 lemon rind
1/2 teaspoon vanilla
1 pinch salt
Butter

Heat milk to boiling and add tapioca stirring with a whisk. Add salt and cook slowly for 10 minutes. Combine egg yolks with sugar in a bowl, add grated lemon rind and vanilla and stir until blended.

Remove tapioca from heat, allow to cool and fold in egg mixture. Butter a mold. Stiffly beat egg whites with a pinch of salt and 3 drops of lemon juice. Fold in prepared mixture and pour in mold. Bake in moderate oven, preferably in bain-marie. Serve with a fruit sauce made by diluting jelly or jam with a little hot water.

STRAWBERRY

ICE

CREAM

TIZIANA

To serve 12 persons
2 pints heavy cream
1 glass milk
1/2 lb sugar
1/2 lb fresh strawberries

Heat milk with sugar to boiling then add heavy cream and stir thoroughly. Continue processing like any other ice cream.

When freezing is almost over, add strawberries previously pressed through a sieve. Serve with small dried cookies.

To vary, use bananas or pineapple instead of strawberries or use shredded marrons glacés reducing sugar to 7 oz.

OCEANIC
CHEESE CAKE

To serve 12 persons

3 lbs Philadelphia Cream cheese
1 lb creamed cottage cheese or ricotta
8 eggs
4 1/2 oz sugar
3 oz heavy cream
3 oz flour

Combine all ingredients in a bowl and mix with a spatula or with a whip until mixture becomes fluffy.

Pie pan lining pastry

1 egg
4 1/2 oz flour
2 oz sugar
2 oz melted butter
1 grated lemon rind or few drops lemon extract

Put flour on pastry board, break egg in center, add sugar, melted butter and lemon rind. Knead well for 3 minutes then roll out dough to 12 inch in diameter. Line pie pan and prebake lining in moderate oven until golden brown.

Take from oven and pour filling. Return to oven and bake for 45 minutes. If during baking top crust becomes too brown, cover it with a sheet of aluminum foil. Remove from oven and let stand in a lukewarm place for 1 hour.

It's good if served at once and even better after one day of storage. Serve with fruit sauces, such as strawberry, cherry, mango, apricot, peach. Sauces can be made either by diluting jellies or jams with hot water or by pressing fresh fruit through a sieve, adding an equal amount of sugar and boiling for 10 minutes.

VANILLA BAVARIAN CREAM

To serve 6 persons

3 egg yolks
4 1/2 oz sugar
1 tablespoon unflavored gelatin
1/2 pint milk
1/2 pint heavy cream
Grated orange rind
2 tablespoons vanilla or 1 vanilla pod

Heat milk to boiling with vanilla pod and grated orange rind. Using powdered vanilla, add it at the end when cream is set out to thicken.

Combine egg yolks and sugar in a bowl. Remove vanilla pod from boiling milk and pour it over eggs mixing until blended. Melt gelatin with 2 tablespoons milk over low heat then fold in mixture and allow to cool. Stir frequently to prevent clot build-up. Meanwhile, whip cream and store in refrigerator. When mixture begins to thicken, fold in whipped cream and transfer into individual molds (or a large one if preferred) and chill in refrigerator for a few hours or until firm. Unmold on serving platter.

To unmold easily, place in lukewarm water for a few seconds.

Serve with whipped cream topping and with candied cherries if desired, or serve it with dried pastry and cookies.

To vary, flavor cream with chocolate adding 1 teaspoon cocoa per person, or with coffee adding 1 teaspoon freshly ground coffee per person. Or line mold with spongy biscuits, of flavor cream half with vanilla and half with chocolate.

IMPERIAL APRICOT SOUFFLE'

To serve 6 persons

12 oz strained apricots
15 oz sugar
1 teaspoon lemon juice
1/2 teaspoon vanilla
8 egg whites
4 1/2 oz peeled sweet almonds
6 fresh apricots
1 glass Kirsh
1 oz butter

Press fresh or canned apricots through a sieve, add sugar lemon juice and vanilla. Cook mixture in a casserole stirring constantly until thickened like a jelly.
Butter a soufflé mold and sprinkle with finely shredded almonds to coat butter completely, then sprinkle with sugar.
Stiffly beat egg whites and fold in prepared cooled jelly. Pour in mold and bake in moderate oven for 1/2 hour. When soufflé is doubled in bulk, remove from oven and garnish with fresh apricot quarters, sprinkle with sugar and bake 5 minutes longer until glazed. Serve at once with apricot sauce flavored with Kirsch.

SURPRISE
OF
MELON
VENTICELLO
DI ROMA

To serve 6 persons

1 large melon
1 small pineapple
2 bananas
2 apples
3 oranges
1/2 lb cherries
1 lb strawberries
4 1/2 oz sugar
1 glass Grand Marnier

Cut a 3/4 inch slice from melon end crosswise so as it can stand. Cut stem side at 3/4 of melon height to form a lid. Scoop out pulp and dice together with bananas, apples and pineapples. Combine in a bowl and add orange segments, stoned cherries cut into halves and 1/2 lb strawberries.
Press remaining strawberries through a sieve to make a purée.
Combine with sugar and liquor and pour on fruit. Mix well and fill melon shell. Cover with reserved slice and chill for at least 2 hours. Serve on a plate with napkin and garnish with green leaves, or place in a bowl with crushed ice.
To vary, use watermelon instead of melon and fill with any fruit in season.

CREPES

BASIS

RECIPE

FOR

UNENDING

VARIATIONS

To prepare 48 crepes about.

1 lb flour
3 oz melted butter
1 dash salt
10 eggs
3 pints milk
2 glasses Cognac or Rum
1 teaspoon vanilla

Heat milk to boiling and allow to cool. Combine flour, salt and eggs in a bowl. Beat with whip until mixture becomes a smooth dough, add vanilla (or any other desired flavoring) liquor, melted butter, mix until blended and fold in milk then let stand for at least 2 hours.

Melt a little butter and reserve in a cup. Brush a 6 inch diameter skillet with melted butter each time, heat and pour 2 tablespoons crepes mixture. Stir so as to form a thin layer evenly spread on bottom of skillet. Fry for 2 minutes then turn with a spatula and allow to cook likewise on other side. Continue until all mixture is used. Delicately arrange fried crepes on a plate.

FAMILIAR
CREPES
SUZETTES

To serve 6 persons

3 oz butter
3 oz sugar
1 tangerine or orange or lemon
1 glass Curaçao
18 crepes (Recipe N. 257)

Beat butter in a bowl until foamy, add tangerine juice, sugar and Curaçao. Mix until well blended.
Prepare crepes and spread with mixture, fold into quarters and arrange on slightly buttered ovenproof serving plate. Dust with vanilla sugar and bake for a few minutes.
Serve at once.

BLINTZES A LA RATTO

To serve 6 persons

1 lb creamed cottage cheese
or ricotta
4 egg yolks
1 pinch cinnamon
2 oz seedless raisins
1 pinch salt
1 grated lemon or orange rind
4 1/2 oz butter
4 1/2 oz sugar
1 lb strawberries
18 crepes (Recipe N. 257)

Begin preparing crepes. Combine creamed cottage cheese, egg yolks, cinnamon, raisins, grated orange rind and salt in a bowl. Mix until well blended. Spread mixture on crepes and fold in quarters.

Press 1/2 lb strawberries through a sieve, add sugar and heat to boiling for 10 minutes preferably in a pyrexware casserole. Remove from heat and fold in remaining strawberries then reserve in a lukewarm place.

Slightly brown prepared crepes in a little butter and serve with strawberry sauce.

To vary, use raspberries or gooseberries.

GOLDEN
PUMPKIN
PIE

To serve 12 to 16 persons

Filling
2 lbs well ripe pumpkin
1 lb sugar
6 eggs
1 pinch salt
1 dash nutmeg
1 pinch ginger
2 lbs heavy cream

Dough
4 1/2 oz melted butter
1 lb flour
4 eggs
Lemon extract
4 1/2 oz sugar

Pastry shell: Combine flour, melted butter, eggs, sugar and a few drops of lemon extract or grated lemon rind. Knead for 3 minutes and roll out just enough to make two 10 inch pastry shells. Prebake in moderate oven until golden brown.
Press pumpkin through a sieve or food chopper, combine with beaten eggs, add salt, ginger, nutmeg, sugar and heavy cream.
Mix well and fill prebaked shells. Bake in moderate oven for 3/4 hour.
Serve lukewarm with slightly sweetened heavy cream flavored with a little vanilla, or serve it cold with whipped cream.

SWEET

JAMAICAN

DREAM

To serve 6 persons

12 marrons glacés
1 glass Jamaican Rum
2 tablespoons sugar
2 glasses Cognac or Brandy
18 crepes (Recipe N. 257)

Coarsely shred marrons glacés and gather in a bowl. Add rum and one tablespoon of butter. Mix well, spread mixture on crepes and fold in quarters. Melt remaining butter in a pan and brown crepes for 2 minutes on each side, dust with sugar, sprinkle with Cognac and ignite.
Serve directly from pan as blazing continues.

CREPES

FAMOUS

MELBA

To serve 6 persons

6 canned peach halves
2 glasses Marsala or Port wine
1 tablespoon arrowroot or cornstarch
3 oz toasted almonds, sweet
1/2 lb raspberries or gooseberries (fresh or frozen)
2 oz sugar
butter
Peach Brandy
18 crepes (Recipe N. 257)

Begin preparing crepes. Cut toasted almonds into thin slices. Cut peach halves into thin slices as well and arrange in pan. Melt cornstarch with Marsala or Port wine and sprinkle on peaches. Heat to boiling constantly stirring. Remove from heat and divide peaches on crepes then roll them up. Butter a pan and arrange rolled crepes.
Press raspberries through a sieve, add sugar and cook for 2 minutes constantly stirring.
Heat pan with rolled crepes, sprinkle with Peach Brandy, coat with strained raspberries and top with toasted almonds.
Cook for 2 minutes and serve at once.

262

CREPES
PUERTORICAN
CAPRICCIO

To serve 6 persons

3 egg yolks
4 1/2 oz sugar
3 teaspoons cornstarch
2 cups strong brewed coffee
1/2 lb fresh or canned pineapple
2 glasses rum
1 oz butter
18 crepes (Recipe N. 257)

Begin preparing crepes. Combine egg yolks, 3 oz sugar and 2 teaspoons cornstarch, mix well with whip and fold in coffee. Heat constantly stirring and allow to cook until thickened. Spread on crepes and fold in quarters. Chop pineapple, add its juice, remaining cornstarch and sugar and heat to boiling for 1 minute constantly stirring.
Butter a pan and arrange crepes, heat and sprinkle with rum, cook for 1 minute then coat with pineapple sauce. Serve at once.

DELICIOUS PINEAPPLE MARIE

To serve 6 persons
1 pineapple
6 1/2 oz vanilla sugar
3 egg yolks
1 pint heavy cream, whipped
2 tangerines

Select a just right pineapple with its stem tuft. Cut off a slice on stem end being careful not to break leaves and reserve to act as lid.

Remove pineapple pulp with a long sharpened knife without slashing rind. Reserve drained juice in a cup. Press half of the pulp through a sieve and dice remaining half then freely sprinkle with sugar.

Combine egg yolks in a pot with remaining sugar, pineapple juice and tangerine juice. Beat for 2 minutes then place pot over low heat or in bain-marie constantly beating. Remove from heat and cool on crushed ice without stopping beating. Fold in strained pineapple, diced pineapple and whipped cream. Pour mixture into pineapple shell and place in freezer for at least 5 hours. Before serving, cover with reserved top slice and place pineapple in a bowl filled with crushed ice. Serve with dried pastry.

FLAMED
BANANAS
LEA

To serve 6 persons

12 small bananas
1 orange
3 oz sugar
1 glass Grand Marnier
1 glass rum

Peel bananas and arrange whole on a plate. Sprinkle with sugar, orange juice and Grand Marnier and let stand for 2 hours to marinate.
Pour in pan and cook over high heat until orange juice is evaporated and sauce thickens. Sprinkle with rum and ignite. Serve at once as blazing continues with small pastry and cookies.

STRAWBERRY
SOUFFLE'
IRRESISTIBLE

To serve 6 persons

1 lb strawberries
3 oz sugar
6 egg whites
1/2 teaspoon vanilla
1/2 lb heavy cream
1 oz vanilla sugar
1 oz butter

Clean fresh strawberries and press through a sieve making
a purée. Combine in a bowl with vanilla and sugar.
Butter six individual molds and dredge with sugar. Stiffly
beat egg whites and gradually fold in strawberry mixture
very delicately. Pour in molds and bake in moderate oven
for 15 minutes. Blend vanilla sugar with lukewarm cream
and coat soufflés. Serve well hot.

FRIED MELON SEGMENTS WITH APRICOT SAUCE

To serve 6 persons

2 lbs melon
2 oz vanilla sugar
1/2 lb flour
2 glasses Maraschino or any other sweet liquor
2 eggs
1 glass white wine or apple juice
1 tablespoon baking powder
1 pinch salt
Oil for frying

Peel and clean melon then cut into segments. Arrange in a pan sprinkle with liquor and sugar and marinate for 1 hour.

Combine flour, eggs, salt, white wine or apple juice in a bowl and mix until of batter consistency. If it becomes too thick add a little water. Add baking powder and mix until dissolved.

Dip melon segments in prepared cream and fry in hot deep oil for 1 minute or until golden brown. Drain and serve.

If desired serve with apricot sauce made by blending apricot jam with hot water or boil strained fresh apricots with an equal amount of sugar for 10 minutes.

SOFT RICE PUDDING WITH CHERRY SAUCE

To serve 6 persons

1/2 lb rice
1 quart milk
1 pinch salt
3 oz vanilla sugar
3 eggs

Sauce
1 lb cherries
2 oz sugar
1 pinch cinnamon
1 glass white wine or apple juice
1 teaspoon cornstarch
1 oz butter

Boil rice in water for 2 minutes. Drain and put it in a casserole, add milk, salt, vanilla sugar, mix and allow to cook for 20 minutes until thickened. Remove from heat and transfer in another container to cool. Fold in egg yolks. Stiffly beat egg whites and fold in with rice mixture. Butter a pudding mold, pour mixture and bake in bain-marie for half hour.

Stone cherries, add cinnamon and sugar and boil for 10 minutes. Blend cornstarch with wine and fold in with cherries. Boil for 1 minutes longer. Remove from heat and store in lukewarm place.

Remove pudding from oven, allow to cool for 5 minutes. Unmold and coat with cherry sauce.

EGGNOG
WITH
MADEIRA
WINE

To serve 3 persons

6 egg yolks
5 1/2 oz sugar
3 glasses Madeira Wine
3 tablespoons water
1/2 teaspoon vanilla

Combine all ingredients in a mixing bowl and beat with a thin wire whip or mixer for 1 minute. Heat in bain-marie constantly whipping until fluffy. Remove from heat and serve in cups with biscuits or pastry.
To vary taste, use Port Wine or Marsala or white wines or liquors or fruit juices.

CONCA D'ORO FRITTERS

To serve 6 persons

1/2 lb flour
2 eggs
3/4 oz yeast
3 oz candied oranges
1 pinch salt
1 glass Curaçao or Cointreau
2 oz vanilla sugar
1 pinch cinnamon
Oil for frying

Combine flour, salt, diced candied oranges, liquor, and eggs in a bowl. Add yeast previously blended in a glass of water. Thoroughly mix for 5 minutes, cover with a napkin and let stand in a lukewarm place for 2 hours to leaven. Drop 1 tablespoon mixture at a time in moderately hot deep oil and fry until swollen and golden brown. Oil must not be too hot otherwise fritters won't fry inside. Drain fritters on a grate and sprinkle with vanilla sugar mixed with cinnamon.

ORANGE
SOUFFLE'
LUNA
ROSSA

To serve 6 persons

6 large oranges
1 pint milk
5 eggs, separated
6 1/2 oz sugar
1 1/2 oz cornstarch
1/2 teaspoon vanilla
1 glass Cointreau or Curaçao

Combine egg yolks, 5 1/2 oz sugar, 1 oz cornstarch and vanilla in a pot. Mix well with whip or mixer, pour boiling milk, heat and cook until boiling is resumed constantly mixing. Remove from heat and transfer in a bowl to cool, occasionally stirring.
Cut oranges crosswise at 3/4 of their heigth. Scoop out pulp without breaking rind. Place oranges upside down on a plate to drain. Press orange pulp through a strainer.
Gather strained pulp in a pot, add drained juice, remaining sugar and cornstarch, liquor and heat for a few minutes constantly stirring until sauce thickens. Stiffly beat egg whites and fold in cooling cream. Fill oranges with cream, arrange on a pan and bake in moderate oven for 15 minutes about. Serve with prepared orange sauce.

PREMIUM STRAWBERRY CUP PAOLA

To serve 6 persons

1 lb strawberries
3 oz vanilla sugar
1/2 pint heavy cream
1 lemon
6 fresh mint leaves
2 glasses Grand Marnier

Clean strawberries, wash them delicately in water with lemon juice. Drain and put in a bowl adding sugar and Grand Marnier. Place in refrigerator for roughly 1 hour.
Remove from refrigerator and transfer well drained in a glass bowl. Take 3 oz strawberries and press them through a sieve together with drained liquor and sugar to make a purée. Fold in whipped cream until well blended. Divide whole strawberries in champagne glasses, top with whipped cream mixture, one mint leaf and a fine whole strawberry.
Serve with small pastry.

272

CHOCOLATE
PROFITEROLLES

1/2 pint water
4 1/2 oz flour
4 1/2 oz butter
4 eggs
1 pinch salt

Combine water, salt and butter in a casserole. Heat to boiling and add flour. Mix with a spatula until smooth, stir 2 minutes longer and remove from heat. Allow to become lukewarm then add eggs one by one constantly stirring for about 5 minutes. Heat oven. Shape balls of mixture large as a walnut and arrange in rows in a buttered shallow baking pan. Bake in hot oven for 10 minutes until dough begins to swell and brown and becomes rather dry. If profiterolles are not sufficiently dry and firm do not remove from oven otherwise they will collapse.
If dough is not used out, repeat the operation always using a cold baking pan. Remove from oven and arrange on a grate or a sieve.

Filling
2 1/2 pints milk
5 1/2 oz flour
11 oz sugar
1 pinch vanilla
1 oz butter
8 egg yolks
1 glass sweet liquor
Combine sugar, flour, egg yolks and vanilla in a casserole and mix well with a whip.
Heat milk to boiling and fold in mixture. Heat and allow to boil for 5 minutes constantly stirring. Remove from heat, add butter and liquor and allow to cool occasionally stirring.
Cut profilerolles with scissors on one side to make an opening large enough to allow filling with 1 teaspoon prepared cream. Arrange filled profiterolles in one or more glass cups and reserve 1/4 of cream for chocolate sauce.

Chocolate sauce

5 1/2 oz chocolate bars
1 glass milk
1/4 profiterolles filling cream

Melt chocolate bars with milk in a casserole over low heat or even better on top of double boiler. Fold in cream and add more milk if too thick.

Coat profiterolles with chocolate sauce; if desired sprinkle shredded toasted hazelnuts and dot with whipped cream.

PAPAYA
PARFAIT
GRANADA

To serve 6 persons

1/2 lb papaya
4 1/2 oz vanilla sugar
12 1/2 oz whipped cream
2 glasses Maraschino
1 glass Cherry Brandy
6 cherries in Maraschino
6 mint leaves

Press ripe papaya through a sieve to make a purée. Add sugar, Maraschino and fold in delicately whipped cream.
Pour into mold and freeze for at least 5 hours. Remove from freezer just before serving. Place mold in water for a few minutes and unmold on serving platter.
Garnish with mint leaves and cherries and sprinkle with Cherry Brandy. Serve with biscuits or dried cookies.

SPECTACULAR
FLAMING
BAKED
ALASKA

To serve 6 or more persons

10 oz strawberry ice cream
10 oz pistacchio ice cream
10 oz chocolate ice cream
Marguerites Cake or Dough
(Currently marketed)
Meringue
Cherries in Maraschino or
other candied fruit
Small tart with 2 lumps of
sugar
1 glass Brandy or Cognac

Marguerite Dough
Although currently marketed, here is the recipe for the preparation of Marguerites, especially suited for Baked Alaska:
3 eggs, separated
5 1/2 oz sugar
4 1/2 oz flour
1 dash salt
1 pinch grated lemon rind or few drops lemon extract
Combine salt, egg yolks and grated lemon rind in a bowl.
Heat to boiling half glass of water and sugar, then pour on egg yolks mixing for 5 minutes. Stiffly beat egg whites and fold in yolks, gradually adding flour constantly stirring until smooth. Butter a pie pan and dredge with flour. Pour mixture and bake in moderate oven for about 30 minutes. Unmold on a sieve or grate. Marguerites may be prepared one day in advance.

Meringue

4 egg whites
3 drops lemon juice
1 dash salt
5 1/2 oz sugar

Meringue should be prepared only shortly before baking Alaska.

Combine egg whites, lemon juice and salt in a bowl. Beat until stiff beginning slowly then gradually increasing speed.

For best results use an electric mixer set first on the lower speed and then switched to higher speed. Fold in sugar and stir until well blended.

Baked Alaska

Pile three layers of ice cream and shape into a brick, or pack in a loaf pan. Place in freezer for a few hours so as ice cream becomes as hard as possible.

Select preferably an oval serving platter. Cut a layer of Marguerites 3/4 inch thick and trim to fit in platter. Sprinkle with a glass of any desired liquor. Arrange ice cream and top with another layer of marguerites, 1/2 inch thick sprinkling it with liquor as well. Entirely coat cake and ice cream with an even layer of meringue 3/4 inch thick. Sprinkle with vanilla sugar and bake in hot oven for a few minutes or until meringue is golden brown. Remove from oven and decorate with cherries in Maraschino or any other candied fruit.

Arrange a small tart on top containing two lumps of sugar and brandy. Ignite and serve immediately as blazing continues.

To vary, select any desired ice cream and proceed as above.

INDEX